Josiah and his Children

Lessons for the Last Generation

Josiah
and his
Children

Lessons for the Last Generation

Stephen Palmer

THE CHRISTADELPHIAN
404 SHAFTMOOR LANE
HALL GREEN
BIRMINGHAM B28 8SZ

2007

First Published 2007

ISBN 978-0-85189-174-3

© 2007 The Christadelphian Magazine and Publishing Association Limited

Printed and bound in England by:

THE CROMWELL PRESS
TROWBRIDGE
WILTSHIRE BA14 0XB

FOREWORD

THE Apostle Paul declared that "whatsoever things were written aforetime were written for our learning, that we through patience and comfort of the scriptures might have hope" (Romans 15:4). As the following pages clearly demonstrate,* the Scripture records of the last days of the old kingdom of Judah contain much that has been "written for our learning": there is encouragement as well as warning, blessing and a bright hope for the future for the faithful, as well as judgement on the wicked. The lessons seem particularly appropriate for our generation which, we believe, is living in the last days prior to the return of Christ.

King Josiah was undoubtedly a remarkable man. Summarising his life, the author observes, "In the words of Lamentations 3:27: 'It is good for a man that he bear the yoke in his youth.' At the tender age of 8 Josiah came to the throne. When he was just 16 years old he began to seek after the God of David his father. At 20 he took up the responsibility of cleansing the land from idolatry. He was rewarded with the discovery of the book of the Law which gave a new strength to his reforms. He humbled himself before the Word of God and turned to Him with all his heart, and soul and strength. He did not deviate from the narrow way and was known not just for zeal but also for his lovingkindness. Certainly it was good that this man took up the yoke in his youth so that he might be an inspiration for us all to follow more diligently the Lord Jesus whom he prefigured" (page 114).

Sadly, his fine example was ignored by the kings who followed – his sons and grandson – all of whom were condemned for doing "evil in the sight of the LORD", even

---

* The material in this book was first published as a series of articles in *The Christadelphian*, from June 1994 to December 1995.

though in two cases they only reigned for three months! The people over whom they ruled preferred to hear the soothing words of false prophets than to listen to the unpalatable truths spoken by men like Jeremiah. In such circumstances the kingdom hurtled towards its own destruction. The same is true of the world in which we are living, and the question posed in the concluding paragraph of this book (page 169) is one we need to ask ourselves: "Shall we be like Jehoahaz or Jehoiakim, Jehoiachin or Zedekiah? Or shall we be like Daniel, Hananiah, Mishael and Azariah, Jeremiah and Ezekiel, people who were brought up in that same generation with the same range of influences bearing in upon them, but who chose a better way?"

ROGER LONG
Birmingham, 2007

CONTENTS

Foreword   … … … … … … … … … … … … … …v

1 An overview   … … … … … … … … … … … …1

2 "Visiting the iniquity of the fathers"   … … … … … …9

3 Time of decision for a teenager   … … … … … … …18

4 Seeking first the kingdom of God   … … … … … …27

5 "Casting down imaginations" … … … … … … … …36

6 Repairing the House of God   … … … … … … … …45

7 Discovering the Word of God … … … … … … … …54

8 Personal discovery of the Word is essential … … …63

9 A new covenant   … … … … … … … … … … …72

10 Vessels fit for destruction   … … … … … … … …81

11 The cleansing continues   … … … … … … … …90

12 The great Passover   … … … … … … … … … …99

13 Josiah as a type of Christ   … … … … … … …108

14 Josiah's children choose death!   … … … … … …116

15 Josiah's son rejects the Word of God … … … … …125

16 Jehoiachin – A despised broken idol?   … … … …134

17 Zedekiah the twilight prince   … … … … … … …143

18 "O Jerusalem, Jerusalem"   … … … … … … …152

19 Shall we learn the lessons? … … … … … … … …161

Index of Scripture References   … … … … … …171

Subject Index … … … … … … … … … … … …177

1

AN OVERVIEW

BY any measure Josiah was an extraordinary person and the times in which he and his children lived were momentous ones in Judah's history. His reign is summarised in glowing terms: "And he did that which was right in the sight of the LORD, and walked in all the way of David his father, and turned not aside to the right hand or to the left" (2 Kings 22:2). The Scriptures related to this period of Judah's history are perhaps less familiar than many other parts of the Bible, but we shall find they contain a wonderful message of the mercy and longsuffering of God set against the most wretched faithlessness of His people.

A Unique King

Josiah was just eight years old when he ascended the throne of Judah in 640 BC, inheriting a kingdom which had been spiritually decimated by the wickedness of his father and grandfather. At the age of sixteen he began to seek after the God of David, and just four years later he embarked upon a massive offensive against the corruption which filled his land. It took him six years to go through the country, pulling down and pulverising the images of idolatry.

At the end of this hectic six year period of reformation, at the time the temple was being renovated a most significant discovery was made. The Law of God was found hidden in the temple. When Shaphan the scribe read it to Josiah it is clear from his reaction that he was hearing that Law being read for the very first time: "And it came to pass, when the king had heard the words of the book of the law, that he rent his clothes" (2 Kings 22:11). This sincere response to hearing the curses of Deuteronomy 28, his humility before the Word of God, and his dedication to following its commandments mark out

1

Josiah as a very special king: "And like unto him was there no king before him, that turned to the LORD with all his heart, and with all his soul, and with all his might, according to all the law of Moses; neither after him arose there any like him" (2 Kings 23:25).

The Scripture just quoted poses a problem to some. The record says that there was no king before or since like Josiah. In other words he was unique. But King Hezekiah is also described in a similar manner. How could two kings be given the same accolade – that there was no king before or since like them? Is Scripture contradicting itself? The answer is that both showed superlative spiritual qualities but in different ways. Hezekiah's commendation was, "He trusted in the LORD God of Israel; so that after him was none like him among all the kings of Judah, nor any that were before him. For he clave to the LORD" (2 Kings 18:5,6). Hezekiah's outstanding quality was the trust he showed when the armies of Sennacherib threatened to overrun Jerusalem. No king before or since under such trial demonstrated such supreme reliance upon God. Josiah's distinction was different. He also demonstrated trust in God but not in the way that Hezekiah did. What marked out Josiah was the way in which he responded to the Word of God. He was moved with a zeal not shown by other kings before or since. It was his "turning" to the Lord which was unique.

The spiritual distinctions afforded to Hezekiah and Josiah do not in any way place these kings on a level with the Lord Jesus Christ. The Master was unique in respect of all spiritual qualities, though bearing the same nature as ourselves. But Josiah, as Hezekiah and other great characters of faith in Scripture, is in so many ways a type of the Lord himself. We should study the life of Josiah not as mere history but as a prophetic portrait of the Master, for this is how the Scriptures present him.

The similarities between Josiah and his greater son, the Lord Jesus Christ, can readily be appreciated when we summarise the life of Josiah as portrayed in Scripture. His coming was predicted by prophecy. He sought the Lord from his youth. Twice he cleansed the temple of idols. In the intervening period he travelled throughout the land, including Israel, to cleanse it of idolatry. During his reign he sought to bring the lost sheep of the house of Israel into the fold of covenant relationship with God. He built up the house of God, in so doing making the Word of God available to the people. He prepared a great passover and he provided the passover lambs. His untimely death at the hands of Gentile powers led to great lamentation amongst his followers. Each of these points when followed through Scripture leads us to the work of the Lord Jesus.

Momentous Times

We need to study Josiah and his children in relation to the times in which he lived. Politically, in the Middle East it was a time of momentous change. The superpower of Assyria was about to collapse. The newly emerging power of Babylon was conspiring with the Medes and the Scythians to topple the Assyrian giant. Egypt, once an enemy of Assyria, was now more worried about the new threat and sought to prop up the crumbling Assyrian as a buffer against Babylon. In this way Egypt sought to establish a suzerainty over Palestine.

In the summer of 612 BC, when Josiah was 36 years old, the combined armies of Babylon and Media attacked and captured the city of Nineveh, the capital of Assyria. The prophecy of Nahum was now fulfilled as the victors put the city to the torch: "The fire shall devour thy bars ... There shall the fire devour thee" (Nahum 3:13,15). Witness to the fulfilment of this Bible prophecy can still be seen today in the British Museum. Wall panels taken from the palace of Sennacherib in Nineveh bear the indelible marks of the fire – and the hand of God.

The Assyrian state survived the destruction of Nineveh for a short time. The king, Ashur-uballit, set up base in Haran but that was also captured in 610 BC. In 609 BC the Assyrian king, with the help of the Egyptians tried to recapture Haran. Pharaoh Necho marched through Josiah's territory on his way to help. When Necho got to Megiddo Josiah went out to fight against him. Despite Necho's protestations Josiah insisted on battle, and even disguised himself in order to engage the enemy. At Megiddo he was hit by the archers and was fatally wounded. Josiah seems to have died in Jerusalem where his servants took him after his injury, and he was buried in one of the sepulchres of his fathers. The prophet Jeremiah led Israel's lamentations over the death of this great king.

Josiah's second son, Jehoahaz, succeeded Josiah, being placed on the throne by the people of Judah. However, he lasted only three months before Pharaoh Necho took him captive to Egypt and placed Jehoahaz's older brother, Jehoiakim, on the throne.

In 605 BC at the battle of Carchemish Assyria was finally defeated and Babylon came to the ascendancy. This was the fourth year of Jehoiakim's reign. Crown Prince Nebuchadnezzar with his army pursued the defeated Egyptians south through the land of Judah. On their way back they took prisoner into Babylon some of the best of the young men of Judah, including Daniel and his friends. A few years later Jehoiakim rebelled against Babylon. Nebuchadnezzar raised a siege against Jerusalem, removed Jehoiakim and took his son Jehoiachin and many others in Judah captive to Babylon. Amongst these captives were Ezekiel and Mordecai. In turn Zedekiah, younger brother of Jehoiakim and Jehoahaz, was placed on the throne by Nebuchadnezzar. He reigned eleven years before he too rebelled against Babylon, provoking the final siege which led to the destruction of the city and the temple in 587 BC.

The Last Generation

The period of time from the reformation of Josiah to the destruction of the temple was only about 40 years, but it is one of the most important periods in the history of God's people. During this period we see one of the fascinating aspects of the Bible. Though its history covers thousands of years the individual books themselves are mainly concentrated into very short periods of time. Seen across the span of human history there were sudden bursts of revelation. The generation of Josiah and his children, short though it was, formed the background for three of the great prophecies of Scripture – Jeremiah, Ezekiel and Daniel, as well as the shorter prophecies of Zephaniah and Habakkuk.

The spiritual characteristics of the last generation of Judah before the Babylonian captivity are described by the contemporary prophets. When we put their prophecies next to the historical accounts in 2 Kings 22–25 and 2 Chronicles 34–36 powerful lessons emerge. We discover that during his short but action-packed life Josiah tried his best to convert the nation to the way of the Lord. But despite his best endeavours his efforts did not succeed. Despite appearances to the contrary the reforms failed to get beneath the surface of the nation. Jeremiah delivers the telling rebuke: "Judah hath not turned unto me with her whole heart, but feignedly, saith the LORD" (3:10).

The seeming failure of Josiah's work should not come as a surprise to us, for in a sense it was inevitable that the reforms would fail. Josiah's grandfather Manasseh had infected the nation so deeply with his idolatrous ways that the disease which surfaced only after Josiah's death was beyond cure. The destruction of Jerusalem, 40 years after the reformation of Josiah, is directly attributed by the prophet Jeremiah to the malign influence of Manasseh: "I will cause them to be removed into all kingdoms of the earth, because of Manasseh the son of Hezekiah king of Judah, for that which he did in Jerusalem" (Jeremiah 15:4). Throughout Josiah's reign the mystery of iniquity was still working in the hearts of the people and their leaders.

It is ironic that nowhere was this evil influence more apparent than in Josiah's own family. The first of his three sons to ascend to the throne reigned just three months, but astonishingly in that short time Jehoahaz developed a reputation for wickedness which was put on record for generations to come: "He did that which was evil in the sight of the LORD, according to all that his fathers had done" (2 Kings 23:32). His brothers Jehoiakim and Zedekiah were no better, though they reigned for longer. Jehoiakim "did that which was evil in the sight of the LORD his God" (2 Chronicles 36:5); and so did Zedekiah who was described by Ezekiel as that "profane wicked prince of Israel" (21:25).

THE LAST GENERATION

Date BC	Kings of Judah	Key Events	Prophets
640	JOSIAH begins reign aged 8 years		
633		JEHOIAKIM born	
632		JOSIAH begins to seek God	ZEPHANIAH - - - -
631		JEHOAHAZ born	
628		JOSIAH begins purge of Jerusalem	
627			JEREMIAH
622		Discovery of the Law, birth of EZEKIEL and? DANIEL, HANANIAH, MISHAEL, AZARIAH	
618		ZEDEKIAH born	
616		JEHOIACHIN born	
612		(fall of Nineveh)	
609	JOSIAH dies, JEHOAHAZ reigns 3 months		
608	JEHOIAKIM begins to reign		
605		(battle of Carchemish) DANIEL, HANANIAH, MISHAEL, AZARIAH to Babylon	
604			DANIEL
598	JEHOIAKIM dies JEHOIACHIN reigns 3 months		
597	ZEDEKIAH begins to reign	JEHOIACHIN, EZEKIEL, MORDECAI to Babylon	
592			EZEKIEL
587		JERUSALEM destroyed	

6

Contrasts and Paradoxes

What we see then in the reign of Josiah are stark contrasts and some searching paradoxes. How was it possible that Josiah, son and grandson of the most malevolent kings in the history of Judah, could at so young an age demonstrate such mature spiritual qualities that marked him out above all other kings of Judah? Bear in mind that the generation in which he was brought up was hopelessly carnal. And how could a man who devoted his life to learning and living the truth of Scripture produce three sons who by their early twenties were thoroughly corrupt? Both questions will be of keen interest to brethren and sisters bringing up children in a world filled with corrupting influences. The earnest desire of every Christadelphian parent is that their children will follow the example of Josiah and not the example of his sons.

Should we say, then, that despite his personal zeal Josiah was a failure? Certainly not. Perhaps the greatest paradox of all is that out of that very generation which was consigned by God to captivity there arose some of the greatest men of faith of all time! In his very own family circle ("of the king's seed", Daniel 1:3), perhaps attending the same Sabbath School and youth group as his own boys, subject to the same influences, there were youngsters such as Daniel, Hananiah and Mishael, who by their mid-teens had developed a faith so strong that they could withstand the fearsome threats of Nebuchadnezzar and quench the violence of fire. Out of what would appear to be similar backgrounds came very different outcomes. This must give us hope and encouragement when we worry about our young people who are subject to such enormous and destructive peer pressure today. But it should also give us cause to beware any sense of complacency regarding our own children. Although there is a sense in which faith can be passed on from one generation to another (2 Timothy 1:5), there is no genetic law which would make this inevitable. Each generation must develop its own faith.

With Daniel and his friends were others also who treasured a legacy from the faithful influence of Josiah. They went into captivity, spared by God for a future work, and there transformed an idolatrous people in one generation into a nation that would never again worship gods of wood and stone and who returned to rebuild the house of God in faith. This has been called the greatest miracle of the book of Daniel, and we can trace its roots to Josiah. Josiah is not to be judged by his influence on his own generation, but by his influence upon later generations who fulfilled the promise implicit in Josiah's very name. Josiah means 'Yah has founded', an inappropriate name for the king if applied to his own time. (Josiah's children were to see the overthrow of the throne of David and the destruction of the holy city and the temple.) But in Josiah the Lord had started a work which would result in the establishment of another house, a house which would rise up out of the rubble of the faithless generation; a house made up of men such as Zerubbabel, Ezra and Nehemiah.

In this respect and in many others Josiah is a wonderful type of the Lord Jesus Christ. We shall find that Josiah's generation has many parallels with our own. May we apply the lessons and exhortations of that last generation to ourselves so that we and our children may, like Daniel and that faithful remnant of Judah, develop the faith which will sustain us in a hostile Gentile world, and bring us to the Kingdom of the Lord and of His Christ.

2

"VISITING THE INIQUITY OF THE FATHERS"

TO understand the way in which the Lord was dealing with Judah during the reign of Josiah and his children we need to go back in time to see the society which Josiah inherited, a society shaped by his grandfather Manasseh. Manasseh, the son of Hezekiah, reigned longer than any other king of Judah, 55 years, and his influence upon the people of Judah was profound. He had a good start in life (with a father who would have been a tremendous example of faith, and a mother, Hephzibah, whose name figured in the prophecies of Isaiah, representing the bride of Christ), yet Manasseh was the worst king Judah ever had: "He did that which was evil in the sight of the LORD, after the abominations of the heathen, whom the LORD cast out before the children of Israel" (2 Kings 21:2).

The comparison with the heathen Canaanites is very significant. It is leading us to consider the fact that it was because of their abominations that God cast the Canaanites out of the land. What else would the Lord do to a people who modelled themselves on the Canaanites!

The Wickedness of Manasseh

A similar line of thought is to be found in the next verse: "For he built up again the high places which Hezekiah his father had destroyed; and he reared up altars for Baal, and made a grove, as did Ahab king of Israel; and worshipped all the host of heaven, and served them" (verse 3). The reference to worshipping "all the host of heaven" is also to be found in 2 Kings 17:16 where the sins of the northern kingdom of Israel are recorded, sins which caused God to eject them also from the land. This was during the reign of Manasseh's father, Hezekiah, and surely Manasseh could not have had a more sober warning of the consequences of idolatry. But just as Ahab had started a process of corruption in Israel which would eventually lead to their downfall, so Manasseh undid all the good his father had done and introduced an apostasy in Judah which could not be corrected by the best efforts of Josiah. Sixty or so years later the Lord would say through the prophet Jeremiah: "I will cause them to be removed into all kingdoms of the earth, because of Manasseh the son of Hezekiah king of Judah, for that which he did in Jerusalem" (Jeremiah 15:4).

The details of the deeds of Manasseh almost defy belief:

"He built altars in the house of the LORD, of which the LORD said, In Jerusalem will I put my name. And he built altars for all the host of heaven in the two courts of the house of the LORD. And he made his son pass through the fire, and observed times, and used enchantments, and dealt with familiar spirits and wizards: he wrought much wickedness in the sight of the LORD, to provoke him to anger. And he set a graven image of the grove that he had made in the house, of which the LORD said to David, and to Solomon his son, In this house, and in Jerusalem, which I have chosen out of all tribes of Israel, will I put my name for ever: neither will I make the feet of Israel move any more out of the land which I gave their fathers; only if they will observe to do according to all that I have commanded them, and according to all the law that my servant Moses commanded them."   (2 Kings 21:4-8)

The record is written in a way which catches the sense of incredulity which the prophets must have felt. It is as if the Scriptures are saying, he committed idolatry, but if that was not bad enough, look where he did it: "He built altars in the house of the LORD, of which the LORD said, In Jerusalem will I put my name." There, "In the house of Yahweh", the most sacred and important place on the face of the earth, he put altars to the worship of the heathen gods, "And he built altars for all the host of heaven in the two courts". The point is repeated again for emphasis: "He set a graven image of the grove ... in the house, of which the LORD said to David, and to Solomon his son, In this house, and in Jerusalem, which I have chosen out of all tribes of Israel, will I put my name for ever ..." Of all the places he could have put it in the land he chose to place it there, in deliberate desecration of the name of the God of Israel who had made such great and precious promises to Manasseh's forebears.*

Into the house of Yahweh Manasseh introduced the gods of Canaan – Baal, the gods of Assyria – "all the host of heaven", and the abominable practice associated with the worship of the Moabite god, Molech, which was to pass living children (his very own sons!) through the sacrificial fire. There in Jerusalem, in the very temple itself, was a heathen ecumenism which would have been unheard of even amongst the heathen nations. Indeed, the measure of the wickedness of Manasseh is quite astonishing: "Manasseh seduced them to do more evil than did the nations whom the LORD destroyed before the children of Israel. And the LORD spake by his servants the prophets, saying, Because Manasseh king of Judah hath done these abominations, and hath done wickedly above all that the Amorites did, which were before him, and hath made Judah also to sin with his idols ..." (2 Kings 21:9-11).

To be worse than the Amorites would seem impossible when we consider the catalogue of perversions Israel were warned against in Leviticus, but Manasseh managed it. Idolatrous worship was but the religious expression of his iniquity. There were also the crimes which betrayed the carnality of man at its worst: "Moreover Manasseh shed innocent blood very much, till he had filled Jerusalem from one end to another" (2 Kings 21:16). Similar deeds are committed today in parts of the world where the fabric of society has collapsed, and from these terrible modern day events we can get some appreciation of what life must have been like in Jerusalem where quite literally the streets would have run with blood.

Forgiveness and the Unforgivable Sin

Given the measure of wickedness the punishment was to be as extreme:

"Therefore thus saith the LORD God of Israel, Behold, I am bringing such evil upon Jerusalem and Judah,

---

* The graven image of the grove was, we understand, a male fertility symbol.

that whosoever heareth of it, both his ears shall tingle. And I will stretch over Jerusalem the line of Samaria, and the plummet of the house of Ahab: and I will wipe Jerusalem as a man wipeth a dish, wiping it, and turning it upside down. And I will forsake the remnant of mine inheritance, and deliver them into the hand of their enemies; and they shall become a prey and a spoil to all their enemies; because they have done that which was evil in my sight, and have provoked me to anger, since the day their fathers came forth out of Egypt, even unto this day." (2 Kings 21:12-15)

Such was the wickedness of Manasseh, a wickedness that could not be removed even by Josiah. His was an indelible blot on the record of Judah. He had defiled the place where God said that His name would dwell and no amount of cleansing by Josiah could remove that stain. In 2 Kings 23, after the magnificent reign of Josiah, after all the cleansing and purging of the land, after the restoration of the temple and the new covenant the people had entered into through his good offices, after the celebration of the passover, after all that wonderful transformation the record says: "Notwithstanding the LORD turned not from the fierceness of his great wrath, wherewith his anger was kindled against Judah, because of all the provocations that Manasseh had provoked him withal. And the LORD said, I will ... cast off this city Jerusalem which I have chosen, and the house of which I said, My name shall be there" (verses 26,27).

And when that fateful day came the Scriptures re-emphasise the reason: "Surely at the commandment of the LORD came this upon Judah, to remove them out of his sight, for the sins of Manasseh, according to all that he did; and also for the innocent blood that he shed: for he filled Jerusalem with innocent blood; which the LORD would not pardon" (2 Kings 24:3,4).

The fact that the great reformation of Josiah failed to make up for the wickedness of Manasseh presents us with something of a problem. Does God store up anger against a people and pour it out on a later generation? In what sense was the sin of Manasseh an unforgivable sin? When we look into this we discover a quite extraordinary turn of events which it is indeed hard to comprehend. Set against the sin which could not be pardoned we find one of the greatest examples of the forgiveness of God. And notice to whom it was offered, to Manasseh himself! To Manasseh, the man who started it all, the man who "filled Jerusalem with blood", desecrating the holy places and leading the people into sins worse than the Amorites – that man!

"Wherefore the LORD brought upon them the captains of the host of the king of Assyria, which took Manasseh among the thorns, and bound him with fetters, and carried him to Babylon. And when he was in affliction, he besought the LORD his God, and humbled himself greatly before the God of his fathers, and prayed unto him: and he was intreated of him, and heard his supplication, and brought him again to Jerusalem into his kingdom. Then Manasseh knew that the LORD he was God." (2 Chronicles 33:11-13)

Forgiveness turned Manasseh's life around and he tried his best to undo the evil that he had done:

"And he took away the strange gods, and the idol out of the house of the LORD, and all the altars that he had built in the mount of the house of the LORD, and in Jerusalem, and cast them out of the city. And he repaired the altar of the LORD, and sacrificed thereon peace offerings and thank offerings, and commanded Judah to serve the LORD God of Israel." (verses 33:15,16)

Unfortunately, as sometimes is the case with us also, Manasseh was unable to undo all that evil. The consequences of his sins continued. For although the people did as the king commanded there is the strong hint that their hearts were not in his reformation. "Nevertheless the people did sacrifice still in the high places, yet unto the LORD their God only" (verse 17).

Who would have thought it possible that a man whose sins lived on for four generations after him in a way which could not be redeemed, would himself find forgiveness with God? What this tells us is that there is no unforgivable sin in the sense which many people seem to conceive of it – that is, a particular sin which in itself is so bad it cannot be forgiven. Every sin known to mankind would have been committed in Jerusalem at this time, because he "did worse than the heathen", and yet Manasseh found forgiveness because he prayed and he intreated and he humbled himself before God.

Understanding the Name of God

Do we then have a contradiction in Scripture, because it says on the one hand that God forgave Manasseh, and on the other that He would not pardon the fact that Jerusalem had been filled with innocent blood? How do we reconcile this dilemma? We need to go to Exodus 34, because the record has made it clear that Manasseh's sins were to do particularly with the name of Yahweh which the king dishonoured when he desecrated the temple. But when Manasseh humbled himself before God and was forgiven the record says that then he knew that Yahweh was God. He came to know from experience what Exodus 34 reveals about the name of God.

The name was revealed to Moses on the mount:

"And the LORD passed by before him, and proclaimed, The LORD, The LORD God, merciful and gracious, longsuffering, and abundant in goodness and truth, keeping mercy for thousands, forgiving iniquity and transgression and sin, and that will by no means clear the guilty; visiting the iniquity of the fathers upon the children, and upon the children's children, unto the third and to the fourth generation."   (Exodus 34:6,7)

What are we to make of this? Is it really saying that Yahweh is prepared to forgive the sinner but must punish someone and chooses to punish the sinner's grandchildren and great grandchildren? How would this demonstrate the justice of God?

Zephaniah's prophecy is helpful here. That prophecy was written during the period of the "last generation" and explains that during the time of Josiah and his children Yahweh was appealing to the people with a longsuffering which the human mind cannot fathom: "I said, Surely thou wilt fear me, thou wilt receive instruction; so their dwelling should not be cut off, howsoever I punished them: but they rose early, and corrupted all their doings. Therefore wait ye upon me, saith the LORD, until the day that I rise up to the prey ..." (Zephaniah 3:7,8).

14

The expression "they rose early" is an important one to note. It is also to be found in Jeremiah 7:13, but there it is used of the Lord Himself. The people "rose early" so that they might practise their wickedness. They wasted no time so that they might get on with the corruption of their lives. But Jeremiah reveals that because the people got up early, the Lord also "rose up early" in the sense of the urgency with which He appealed to them through the prophets to try to turn the people to repentance: "And now, because ye have done all these works, saith the LORD, and I spake unto you, rising up early and speaking, but ye heard not; and I called you, but ye answered not ..."

When we come to the summary of the period given in 2 Chronicles 36 we realise that this appeal was not limited to one or two occasions; it was for three or four generations:

> "Moreover all the chief of the priests, and the people, transgressed very much after all the abominations of the heathen; and polluted the house of the LORD which he had hallowed in Jerusalem. And the LORD God of their fathers sent to them by his messengers, rising up betimes (early), and sending; because he had compassion on his people, and on his dwelling place: but they mocked the messengers of God, and despised his words, and misused his prophets, until the wrath of the LORD arose against his people, till there was no remedy."   (2 Chronicles 36:14-16)

Here is the explanation for the "three and four generations". Four generations after Manasseh Babylon came against Jerusalem, not because God had stored up His anger against Manasseh and was now going to vent it on his children, but because after that period of time, the Lord could do no more to bring the people to repentance. The people had willingly followed the wicked ways of Manasseh, and though he repented and turned to the Lord they did not. They had every opportunity, especially during the reign of Josiah. The example was there, and the environment had been created to foster faithfulness; there was even the new impetus in the discovery of the Law. But the people in general did not want to know and so there was no remedy.

"The longsuffering of our Lord is salvation"

Rather than thinking of "visiting the iniquity of the fathers upon the children" as a mark of the severity of God's judgements we should see it as a measure of His forbearance, as He waited and waited and waited, not willing that any should perish but that all should come to repentance. In this particular respect the times of Josiah were just like the times of the Lord Jesus Christ and the apostles. In Daniel 9 the 70 Weeks prophecy made clear 490 years before the Lord Jesus that Judah and Jerusalem were to be destroyed. During the last week of years of this prophecy the nation had the greatest possible witness to the compassion and love of God revealed in the Lord, and they had the witness of the Holy Spirit through the Master and the apostles, but still they refused to hear.* The inevitable result was that when the 70 weeks of years were expired the city and the sanctuary would be destroyed.

Yet that destruction did not come immediately, though it was certain to come. In the timescale of the prophecy the crucifixion occurred in the middle of the last week, leaving just three-and-a-half days of years of witnessing by the apostles before the time had run out. Probably this brings us to the time of the death of Stephen. But judgement did not come for another 40 years or so. During all this time God waited. For the people of Judah it was borrowed time, although they paid little attention to the prophecy. It was a measure of the longsuffering and mercy of God, but many took it as evidence that the apostles were wrong in their predictions. We believe this is what Peter is referring to in his Second Epistle. It was not that God was "slack concerning his promise". Peter explains that they should "account that the longsuffering of our Lord is salvation" (3:15). Eventually the judgement did come and Jerusalem was trodden down of the Gentiles.

What a lesson for us today. We are living in the "last generation". The overthrow of the kingdoms of men is certain, but we do not know how soon that judgement will

---

* We shall see as the study progresses that the Master's thoughts in the days leading up to his crucifixion often focused upon the times of Josiah and his sons.

come. We can look back to Josiah's time and see that their day of reckoning took just 40 years, the same period of time from the crucifixion to AD 70, but the people did not know how long they had to wait. Many did not believe it would come at all and accepted the reassurance of the false prophets. We have already waited 40 years since the establishment of the State of Israel. The kingdom has not yet come. Are there doubting hearts who wonder if it will ever come? Is there a feeling that the Lord is slack concerning his promises? The right way to understand the period in which we are privileged to live now is to consider that we are recipients of the longsuffering of God, and to redeem the time. Let us learn from Josiah and take his example. We will see that here was a man in a hurry. He knew what had to be done and he wasted no time in doing it.

3

TIME OF DECISION FOR A TEENAGER

"Josiah was eight years old when he began to reign, and he reigned in Jerusalem one and thirty years. And he did that which was right in the sight of the LORD, and walked in the ways of David his father, and declined neither to the right hand, nor to the left. For in the eighth year of his reign, while he was yet young, he began to seek after the God of David his father: and in the twelfth year he began to purge Judah and Jerusalem from the high places, and the groves, and the carved images, and the molten images."

(2 Chronicles 34:1-3)

WHAT a remarkable testimony to the possibilities of youth! Here is an example which every Christadelphian parent would love their child to follow. The truth is, though, that so many parents are disappointed. Even children brought up in the best of spiritual environments may rebel when they reach the teenage years. How much more remarkable that Josiah, whose father and grandfather had set the worst examples, could, by the age of 16 years, demonstrate such spiritual strength of character. Some teenagers turn completely away from the Truth but do eventually in later years come to their senses – and then have to worry about their own children! Others zealously embrace the Truth initially but fall away when they are exposed to the influences of the wider world. In Josiah we have a young man who both began with zeal and sustained his commitment throughout his life.

What do the Scriptures reveal about the influences which operated upon this young man's mind and how he responded to them?

Grandfather Manasseh

Josiah would have known his grandfather for the first six years of his life, long enough to get a lasting memory. What sort of influence would Manasseh have been?

We have seen that the latter part of the life of Manasseh was a witness to the mercy of God, so great in its scope that it defies human logic. Yet that is the mercy which is memorialised in His great and holy name. Manasseh's repentance and conversion is perhaps the most stunning in the whole of Scripture. He turned from being the leader of an apostasy which was worse than the Canaanites of old to become an example of prayerful humility, an example which was to be recorded for later generations. We are not told how long Manasseh reigned in this new state of mind. He had time enough to take down the idols which were in the house of the Lord, to repair His altar in the temple and to undertake major building work in Jerusalem. The people were made to offer sacrifices to Yahweh only.

It would seem probable that as part of his reformation Manasseh, in his new state of repentance, would have tried to influence his grandson for good, creating an environment conducive to spiritual growth, ensuring that wise counsellors took responsibility for his education and nurturing. So, surprising as it may seem when we just consider the account in 2 Kings of the wickedness of Manasseh, it is likely that Manasseh was actually an influence for good in his personal relationship with Josiah.

This influence would be reinforced upon the mind of Josiah when he read the records of state of the house of David. Reference is made to two separate written accounts of the conversion of Manasseh which must be in addition to the 2 Chronicles account. There is a reference in 2 Chronicles 33:18 which speaks of "the rest of the acts of Manasseh, and his prayer unto his God, and the words of the seers that spake to him in the name of the LORD God of Israel, behold, they are written in the book of the kings of Israel". This cannot be exactly the same book that we know as 2 Kings since no mention is made there of Manasseh's conversion. There must have been other records and indeed other prophets of Yahweh that we are not told about. A second record is mentioned in the next

19

verse, "His prayer also, and how God was intreated of him, and all his sin, and his trespass, and the places wherein he built high places, and set up groves and graven images, before he was humbled: behold, they are written among the sayings of the seers" (verse 19).

Father Amon

Certainly, Manasseh's conversion did not have any positive effect upon his own son Amon. Amon was twenty-two years old when he began to reign, and he had reigned just two years when his servants killed him in his own house. During that time all the Scripture record says of him is that: "He did that which was evil in the sight of the LORD, as did Manasseh his father: for Amon sacrificed unto all the carved images which Manasseh his father had made, and served them; and humbled not himself before the LORD, as Manasseh his father had humbled himself; but Amon trespassed more and more" (2 Chronicles 33:22,23). The record in 2 Kings 21:22 adds that he "forsook the LORD God of his fathers, and walked not in the way of the LORD".

The latter reference to Amon *forsaking* the way of the Lord suggests that he had been brought up in that way by his father. One can imagine that with the zeal of the convert Manasseh would have done as much as he could to ensure that his son did not follow his earlier example. But he was unsuccessful. Perhaps the humility of Manasseh was interpreted by Amon as weakness, and Amon was much more inclined to take notice of the reputation his father had earned when he was young.

No doubt there would be no shortage of discontented people wanting to tell Amon in great detail what his father was once like. The people in general would have greeted Manasseh's about turn with utter dismay. He had done a very thorough job in the first place in turning them to idolatry, overcoming the magnificent influence of Hezekiah, and sinking to a level of corruption unsurpassed by the heathen. How could anyone expect the sudden change of heart of the king to have any significant effect upon the hearts of the people? Brethren and sisters may have a similar experience with their children who are like Amon, unimpressed with the recent change of heart of

20

their parents and very much more inclined to follow the example of former associates.

The record suggests that Amon did more than just follow the crowd, however. Amon "sacrificed to all the carved images which Manasseh his father had made". These images had probably been cast out of the city (2 Chronicles 33:15) by Manasseh during his reformation. Who had rescued and stored them? Had they been preserved like ancient works of art are today kept as treasures? When Manasseh was dead they were quickly brought back into use. We shall see that in the reign of Josiah a similar course of events was prevented in the most emphatic way. Josiah deliberately broke up and crushed to powder all offending idols!

The reference to Amon trespassing "more and more" brings to mind the description which the Apostle Paul gives to Timothy of the "last days", when he says that "evil men and seducers shall wax worse and worse, deceiving, and being deceived" (2 Timothy 3:13). Amongst the catalogue of the characteristics of the men which make the times perilous for the saints Paul cites "disobedient to parents" as one of them. Children, we may say, have always tested their parents' resolve, and tended to push against their parents' restraining counsel, and that may be so. But here in the letter to Timothy (and also in Romans 1:30 where being "disobedient to parents" is a feature of a reprobate world), much more is involved.

Such a trend is very evident throughout Western society today where the youth culture, unknown in previous generations, is degenerating into anarchy and self-destruction. Most of the street crime and the pitiless violence against the elderly and the helpless is committed by young people, often to feed their addictions to drugs. The cause of this trend is no doubt very complex in human terms, and widely debated by politicians and social scientists, but one of the key factors must be the breakdown of discipline within the family and the lack of respect of children for parents.

Proverbs predicts such a generation which has thrown off the restraint of its parents and has descended to moral bankruptcy. The description it gives begins in a way which highlights the significance of obedience to parents:

"There is a generation that curseth their father, and doth not bless their mother. There is a generation that are pure in their own eyes, and yet is not washed from their filthiness. There is a generation, O how lofty are their eyes! and their eyelids are lifted up. There is a generation, whose teeth are as swords, and their jaw teeth as knives, to devour the poor from off the earth, and the needy from among men." (Proverbs 30:11-14)

This description may have been fulfilled more than once during the history of God's people. It certainly was going to be fulfilled in the last generation before the overthrow of Jerusalem. This can be seen by following through the records of that generation in the prophecies of Ezekiel and Jeremiah. For example, Ezekiel says of Jerusalem at that time: "In thee have they set light by father and mother: in the midst of thee have they dealt by oppression with the stranger; in thee have they vexed the fatherless and the widow" (Ezekiel 22:7). A later verse in the same chapter goes on to describe the false prophets as having sharpened teeth to devour: "There is a conspiracy of her prophets in the midst thereof, like a roaring lion ravening the prey" (verse 25). With respect to the description in the Proverbs about that generation being pure in their own eyes, Jeremiah says, "Yet thou sayest, Because I am innocent, surely his anger shall turn from me. Behold, I will plead with thee, because thou sayest, I have not sinned" (Jeremiah 2:35).

Could there be elements of the description in Proverbs fulfilled in the ecclesia of Christ in the generation which will see his return? How important it is for ecclesias and families in the Lord to create and cultivate the spirit of respect for elders. Parents' respect for their own parents is one of the best examples young people could have. It will be hard work, an uphill struggle, because peer pressure and the influence of the media and the youth culture on our young people can be so strong. What must not happen is for the older ones to capitulate to fashionable theories and become frightened to assert scriptural principles of discipline in the home and in the ecclesia for fear that it will put off our young people. We must be true to God's Word and trust that the wisdom revealed in it will accomplish its intended purpose.

A generation gap is there to be seen in many ecclesias. How many fraternal gatherings are attended almost exclusively by the middle-aged and elderly, and the young people organise their own activities? The ecclesia needs to take its responsibility for youth groups and youth gatherings seriously and provide sound scripturally-based leadership. Perhaps the problem for Manasseh was that he did not start educating Amon in the ways of God early enough. Sadly, some brethren and sisters today will feel that they have woken up to the importance of scriptural leadership in the home too late to have much effect upon the thinking of their children.

As far as Josiah was concerned, his father Amon did not reign long enough to have much influence upon him after Manasseh's death. By the time he ascended to the throne Josiah was in the care of wise guardians.

Mother Jedidah

All we are told of Josiah's mother is her name and the name of her father. She was "Jedidah, the daughter of Adaiah of Boscath" (2 Kings 22:1). There is a beauty in the meaning of these names which if it reflected the character of Josiah's mother would mean that she was certainly an influence for good. "Jedidah" means 'beloved', and "Adaiah" means 'Yah has adorned'. The very fact that mothers of the kings of Judah are so often mentioned suggests that they had a considerable influence, as we would expect, on the development of their sons.

Cousin Zephaniah

With regard to other relatives who might have had a formative influence upon Josiah we should consider the prophet Zephaniah. Zephaniah's ancestry is given at the beginning of his prophecy. He was the "son of Cushi, the son of Gedaliah, the son of Amariah, the son of Hizkiah" (Zephaniah 1:1). The name "Hizkiah" in the original Hebrew text is identical with the name also translated "Hezekiah". It would seem likely that this was the great King Hezekiah, the great-grandfather of Josiah, otherwise there would seem little point in giving the genealogy. If this is the case, Zephaniah would be a cousin of Josiah and would in all probability have been brought up in close proximity to Josiah in the royal palace. So even though society at large was hostile to the things of God at that time in Jerusalem, there would have been some young people who could have offered good and wholesome companionship for the young king. The prophecy of Zephaniah was probably given early on in the reign of Josiah and so would have been a major stimulus to Josiah to seek after the God of David his father.

Counsellors and Friends*

When Josiah came to the throne he had at his side two counsellors who supported his reforms and in all probability were the guides who steered him in the right direction. Hilkiah the high priest and Shaphan the scribe discovered the copy of the Law of Moses in the temple when they were supervising the repairs. They were leaders of the delegation which Josiah sent to Huldah the prophetess to enquire of the Lord, and Hilkiah was put in charge of the second and more thorough purging of idolatry from Jerusalem. There are other servants mentioned with Hilkiah and Shaphan suggesting that providentially the Lord provided sound support for the young king.

Jeremiah the prophet was the son of Hilkiah. If, as seems likely, it was the same Hilkiah who was the high priest, then Jeremiah who began his career as a prophet at a very young age (see Jeremiah 1:6) would have been about the same age as Josiah. As the son of such an important figure in Jerusalem, Jeremiah would probably have been brought up with Josiah in the same privileged circle of the royal court. It is not fanciful to think of Josiah attending the same Sabbath School and the same 'youth circle' as Jeremiah and Zephaniah. In addition, there is also Ahikam to be considered. Ahikam, who defended Jeremiah in the reign of Jehoiakim (Jeremiah 26:24), was the son of Shaphan the scribe and was part of the

* For a detailed account of "The Friends of Jeremiah", see Brother Tony Benson's articles in *The Testimony*, November 1972 to May 1973.

delegation which was sent by Josiah to Huldah. He would have been another in a remarkable circle of young people.

One of the surprise characters who appears in the record of Josiah's reign is the prophetess Huldah. It was to her that Josiah sent his deputation after the discovery of the Law. This is in itself surprising since the Law was discovered in the eighteenth year of his reign and Jeremiah the prophet had been prophesying since the thirteenth year of his reign. Why didn't Josiah send to Jeremiah for advice? Huldah was married to Shallum, who held the post, "keeper of the wardrobe". This was presumably a position at court. This means that Huldah and Shallum were probably part of that group of people whose godly influence helped the young Josiah grow up into the sort of king he was".*

Individual Choice

All these definite and possible influences which we are able to identify from the Scriptures of course only give us part of the picture. It is clear from the accounts in the prophets that these few godly characters were exceptions to the rule in Jerusalem. Surrounding the young king were a multitude of evil influences and temptations which could easily have led him along the broad way to destruction which his father had followed. There was nothing inevitable about Josiah's course in life. Josiah had to choose which influences to follow. He had to decide to listen to wise counsel in order that by the age of sixteen he was in a position to make a choice to seek after God.

Sixteen is often a critical age for young people today. A young person typically has just emerged from the physical transition from childhood to adulthood which is often a stressful time for both the young person and the parents! Intellectually he or she is quite capable of grasping the basic tenets of the Truth and there is often an idealism and keenly developed conscience, so that sixteen or thereabouts is not an unusual age of baptism for those who have been brought up in the Truth. Nevertheless maturity is some way off and all our young people need

* Ibid., March 1973, page 94.

close support from older brethren and sisters, even after they are baptized.

Because sixteen is rightly considered a young and tender age we sometimes hear the argument that it is too young to be baptized. It is even suggested that young people need to have a wider experience of the world before they are in a position to make the choice to follow the Lord. Whilst we should rightly avoid pressuring our young people to be baptized before they are themselves ready to make their own decisions, how dangerous is the advice which advocates that a young person should put off his decision until he has seen what life has to offer! Solomon describes the ultimate in this sort of search for experience. He says, "I said in my heart, Go to now, I will prove thee with mirth ... to give myself unto wine ... to lay hold on folly ... I made me great works; I builded me houses; I planted me vineyards: I made me gardens and orchards ... I made me pools of water ... I got me servants and maidens ... I gathered me also silver and gold ... I gat me men singers and women singers ... musical instruments ... and whatsoever mine eyes desired I kept not from them, I withheld not my heart from any joy ... and, behold, all was vanity and vexation of spirit" (Ecclesiastes 2:1-11).

Would we really suggest that our young people should follow this example? Do we all have to experience folly before we can conclude that it really is folly? Can we never learn from the mistakes of others? Solomon's conclusion is very different: "Remember now thy Creator in the days of thy youth" (Ecclesiastes 12:1) is without doubt the right approach. "It is good for a man that he bear the yoke in his youth", says Jeremiah (Lamentations 3:27), and he knew what he was talking about. May the example of Josiah be an inspiration to all our young people to heed this counsel.

4

SEEKING FIRST THE KINGDOM OF GOD

WE have suggested that Josiah would have been brought up as a child in a spiritual atmosphere deliberately fostered by his grandfather Manasseh, and nurtured by his mother and other counsellors, including Hilkiah the high priest and Shaphan the scribe. But one of the most significant of all possible influences would have been missing, and that was knowledge of the Law of Moses.

We can infer that the Law was not available to him because when the copy was discovered in the temple by Hilkiah and read by Shaphan to the king, he was dismayed at its contents. It is obvious that this was the very first time he had heard those words. How much of the remaining Scriptures were available to Josiah we cannot say with certainty, but it would seem likely that the records of the house of David would have been preserved,* including the books of Kings and maybe the rest of the Scriptures which had been written up to that time; it was only the Law of Moses that we are told was rediscovered.

Seeking the God of David His Father

There must have been some access to the Word of God, whether written or verbal, because when Josiah was just sixteen years old he "began to seek after the God of David his father" (2 Chronicles 34:3), and he was successful. Not only so, but having found the God of David, he "did that which was right in the sight of the LORD, and walked in all the way of David his father, and turned not aside to the right hand or to the left" (2 Kings 22:2).** Josiah must therefore have had access to knowledge of that way.

---

* For example, see the references to the chronicles of Manasseh's reign in 2 Kings 21:17 and 2 Chronicles 33:18,19.
** Josiah may have been helped through special revelations from the prophets such as Huldah whom he consulted after the Law had been discovered.

The references to Josiah seeking the "God of David", and walking "in all the way of David", and the repeated description of David as Josiah's "father", give a particular emphasis to Josiah's endeavour. The phrase, "God of David", occurs in only two other passages, 2 Kings 20:5 and Isaiah 38:5. Both of these passages are about the same incident in the reign of Hezekiah. Hezekiah had been told by Isaiah that his disease was terminal and that he should set his house in order in preparation. There was a special irony in that remark because Hezekiah's house could not be set in order at that time! Hezekiah had no heir, and it was only the extension of 15 years of life which enabled the line of succession to the throne of David to continue through his son Manasseh. No doubt it was the threat to the house of David and to the fulfilment of the promises concerning the seed of David which so upset Hezekiah. The king's prayer was heard by God who answered him with the words of Isaiah: "Thus saith the LORD, the God of David thy father, I have heard thy prayer ... and I will add unto thy days fifteen years ... for mine own sake, and for my servant David's sake" (2 Kings 20:5,6). When the same phrase is applied to Josiah, it is underlining the great significance which Josiah must have been placing upon his spiritual heritage.

"In the way of David"

A similar point is raised by the use of the expression, "the way of David" (2 Kings 22:2). The only other occurrence of this phrase is in 2 Chronicles 11:17 where it refers to the first three years of the reign of Rehoboam, after the secession of the northern ten tribes under the leadership of Jeroboam: "So they strengthened the kingdom of Judah, and made Rehoboam the son of Solomon strong, three years: for three years they walked in the way of David and Solomon." The subject of the verse is the priests, Levites and other faithful in the ten tribes who allied themselves with Rehoboam and the worship of God at Jerusalem. The repetition of the phrase "the way of David" in the reign of Josiah again underlines Josiah's appreciation of the significance of his heritage, the throne of David.

As Josiah learned the history of his own royal family he must have been deeply impressed with the faith of David

28

and the great and precious promises which God had made to him. Bearing this in mind, Josiah presents to us an excellent example of what the Lord Jesus Christ requires of us all: "Seek ye first the kingdom of God, and his righteousness." Few kings followed that example. An example of a king who did not was Josiah's own son Jehoiakim who used his privileged position to satisfy the lusts of the flesh. Jeremiah rebuked Jehoiakim by contrasting him with his father, Josiah. Jeremiah says:

> "Shalt thou reign, because thou closest thyself in cedar? Did not thy father eat and drink, and do judgment and justice, and then it was well with him? He judged the cause of the poor and needy; then it was well with him: was not this to know me? saith the LORD. But thine eyes and thine heart are not but for thy covetousness." (Jeremiah 22:15-17)

No doubt luxuries would have been available to Josiah if he had so wished, but all that Jeremiah says is that he ate and drank, which emphasises the basic necessities of life which the Father will provide for us if we first seek His Kingdom. Josiah had set his heart on better things – to find out and to get to know the God who had so inspired his illustrious forebear. The same principle applies today. To follow after and find the spiritual treasures, we shall have to make sacrifices of fleshly things. It is often a straight choice of what to do with the kingly luxury of time.

Warning against Apostasy

Did Josiah have access to what we know as 1 Kings 13? We cannot be sure but it seems probable. This chapter recounts the incident in which the "man of God" tells Jeroboam the son of Nebat that there would arise a man by the name of Josiah who would tear down the altars of idolatry at Bethel. When Josiah fulfilled that prophecy he came across the sepulchre of the "man of God": "Then he said, What title is that that I see? And the men of the city told him, It is the sepulchre of the man of God, which came from Judah, and proclaimed these things that thou hast done against the altar of Bethel. And he said, Let him alone; let no man move his bones" (2 Kings 23:17,18). The record reads as if Josiah was unsurprised by the answer

29

and knew full well what the men were talking about. If this was the case it suggests that Josiah as he grew up would know, and so would his mentors, that he was a child of promise with a special mission. It would also mean that the lessons of 1 Kings 13 would have been the subject of his keenest interest.

The incident recorded in 1 Kings 13 was a dramatic denouncement of the new apostasy which Jeroboam was setting up in Bethel. Jeroboam was frightened that if the ten tribes continued to go to Jerusalem to worship at the temple, then they would eventually rebel against Jeroboam and return to the house of David. To counter this Jeroboam invented a new religion. He took two "calves of gold" and said: "Behold thy gods, O Israel, which brought thee up out of the land of Egypt" (1 Kings 12:28), as Aaron had done at the foot of Mount Sinai. One calf was set up in Dan and the other in Bethel. He instituted a new priesthood, "and made priests of the lowest of the people, which were not of the sons of Levi" (verse 31); and he created a new festival instead of the feast of tabernacles, "a feast in the eighth month, on the fifteenth day of the month, like unto the feast that is in Judah" (verse 32).

Jeroboam himself seems to have taken on the role of high priest because the record says: "... and he offered upon the altar. So did he in Bethel, sacrificing unto the calves that he had made: and he placed in Bethel the priests of the high places which he had made. So he offered upon the altar which he had made in Bethel the fifteenth day of the eighth month, even in the month which he had devised of his own heart; and ordained a feast unto the children of Israel: and he offered upon the altar, and burnt incense" (verses 32,33). The repetition in these verses of the phrase, "which he had made", and the description of the feast as one which "he had devised *of his own heart*" make the point of the record quite clear. Here was a man-made religion, created quite deliberately to counter the true. As such it stands as representative of all human religions, and what happened to Jeroboam is telling us what the One True God thinks of such institutions.

Prophecy of Josiah

The message against Jeroboam from God came at the most dramatic moment possible, as he stood at the altar he had made to offer incense at the inaugural ceremony. With all his people gathered around, and no doubt with great pomp and circumstance, he ascended the platform to offer incense and initiate a system of religion which "became a sin". Just as the moment came to offer the incense the studied solemnity was shattered as a man in the crowd shouted out: "O altar, altar, thus saith the LORD; Behold, a child shall be born unto the house of David, Josiah by name; and upon thee shall he offer the priests of the high places that burn incense upon thee, and men's bones shall be burnt upon thee" (1 Kings 13:2).

It is interesting that the words spoken by the "man of God" were not directed to Jeroboam himself but to the altar. The denunciation was not merely of Jeroboam the man, but of the system of religion which he was trying to establish. As Jeroboam stretched out his hand to command his officers to arrest the prophet, his hand withered and the joints seized up. At the same time "the altar was rent, and the ashes poured out from the altar, according to the sign which the man of God had given by the word of the LORD" (verse 5). It was a telling witness. Offering up incense was a symbol of prayer (Psalm 141:2). Jeroboam could never offer acceptable prayer if he was worshipping through a system which he had devised himself. Surely this emphasises to us that our worship can only be accepted by God if it is based upon the truth of His Word. The doctrinal basis of our faith is critical to the acceptability of our prayers and praise.

The Man of God

The name of the "man of God" who came out of Judah is not recorded. Clearly it is not relevant. What is important is that he was speaking the word of the Lord. In that chapter the phrase "word of the LORD" is used ten times. (In the whole of the books of Kings it is used only 48 times.) The prepositions which introduce the phrase also are unusual. The phrase "*by* the word of the LORD" is used six times in this chapter, and only three times in the rest of the AV. The emphasis could hardly be more powerful. He

31

cried unto the altar "in the word of the LORD". His identity is lost in the power of the words he conveyed. Only through that Word could acceptable prayer be offered. Jeroboam, unable to offer incense himself, pleads with the man of God: "Intreat now the face of the LORD thy God, and pray for me, that my hand may be restored me again. And the man of God besought the LORD, and the king's hand was restored him again, and became as it was before" (1 Kings 13:6).

This association between the "man of God" and the Word of God is interesting in relation to the only two occurrences of the phrase in the New Testament. Both occasions are in Paul's letters to Timothy. As in 1 Kings 13 the first occurrence contrasts the "man of God" with apostasy. Paul says, "For the love of money is the root of all evil: which while some coveted after, they have erred from the faith, and pierced themselves through with many sorrows. But thou, O man of God, flee these things" (1 Timothy 6:10,11).

Paul has earlier identified the motivation for setting up new forms of worship and inventing new doctrines which are not taught in Scripture:

"If any man teach otherwise, and consent not to wholesome words, even the words of our Lord Jesus Christ, and to the doctrine which is according to godliness; he is proud, knowing nothing, but doting about questions and strifes of words, whereof cometh envy, strife, railings, evil surmisings, perverse disputings of men of corrupt minds, and destitute of the truth, supposing that gain is godliness: from such withdraw thyself." (verses 3-5)

Here is religion as Jeroboam would have it, created by men for their own selfish ends; cleverly constructed, as judged by human reasoning, but devoid of the truth which comes only from the revealed Word of God.

"The man of God" represents the very opposite of these things, a person in whom the wholesome words of the Lord are developing a Christlike character which gives glory to the Father. And of course this is the purpose God has in revealing His Word. Paul goes on to explain to Timothy in his second epistle:

"Continue thou in the things which thou hast learned and hast been assured of, knowing of whom thou hast learned them; and that from a child thou hast known the holy scriptures, which are able to make thee wise unto salvation through faith which is in Christ Jesus. All scripture is given by inspiration of God, and is profitable for doctrine, for reproof, for correction, for instruction in righteousness: that the man of God may be perfect, throughly furnished unto all good works."

(2 Timothy 3:14-17)

Fellowship and False Worship

Though Jeroboam offered hospitality and reward for the mercy shown, the man of God refused. He had been commanded "by the word of the LORD" not to go in to Jeroboam's house, and not to eat or drink in Bethel. He was to withdraw himself from any association with the false system at Bethel, even to the point of taking a different way home to Judah (1 Kings 13:9). The path from Judah to Bethel must not become well trodden! But on his way back to Judah he was overtaken by the old prophet who was desperate for fellowship with a man of God. The old prophet had been told by his sons about the events at the altar. The fact that he was not there himself suggests that he was not a supporter of this new religion and seemed quite genuine in his desire to talk with a like-minded man. He offered hospitality in his home.

At first the man of God refused. The reason was the same as that given to Jeroboam. But then the old prophet fabricated a story which changed the man of God's mind: "He said unto him, I am a prophet also as thou art; and an angel spake unto me by the word of the LORD, saying, Bring him back with thee into thine house, that he may eat bread and drink water. But he lied unto him" (verse 18). The lie was convincing. The man of God was tired. (He had been found "sitting under an oak".) He accepted the hospitality. At the meal table the word of the Lord really did come to the old prophet and "he cried unto the man of God that came from Judah, saying, Thus saith the LORD, Forasmuch as thou hast disobeyed the mouth of the LORD, and hast not kept the commandment which the LORD thy God commanded thee, but camest back, and hast eaten bread and drunk water in this place, of the which the LORD did say to thee, Eat no bread, and drink no water; thy carcase shall not come unto the sepulchre of thy fathers" (verses 21,22).

God's Hand at Work

On his way home to Judah the man of God was attacked by a lion and killed. Passers-by saw an extraordinary sight: the body of the man of God lying in the path, with the lion, and the ass he had been riding standing next to the carcase. What could such things mean? Word got back to the old prophet who went to see for himself. The animals were still there and the lion had not eaten the carcase or attacked the ass. Here, in the muzzling of the lion and the calming of the ass was miraculous evidence that the hand of God was at work.

The lesson from this incident is powerful. We can readily see that fellowship with the apostate religion of Jeroboam was completely unacceptable, but was it really so bad to accept the brief hospitality of the old prophet? After all, should we not take every opportunity to encourage those who are seeking the truth? Perhaps we may feel a little sympathy for the old prophet who was looking for friendship with a man of God out of Judah. But if he had really wanted fellowship on God's terms he could have done what it seems many others had done in Israel and left their possessions to sojourn in Judah (2 Chronicles 11:14). Perhaps the man of God had felt this same sympathy. We may feel that the man of God was harshly treated, but the Scriptures are teaching us that the first and overriding priority is to remain faithful to the Word of God. It is not for us to follow Jeroboam and compromise God's way.

Hold On to the Faith

The man of God had been deceived by the lie that there had been a new revelation from God which contradicted the previous revelation he had received. The same thing can happen today. We can be challenged by new erroneous interpretations of Scripture which contradict our faith. We are surrounded by "christians" who claim direct revelation from God through the Holy Spirit, yet they still do not accept the simple truths of Scripture or its authority. We must not be beguiled by these things, but we must hold on to the faith once delivered unto the saints.

There is the view that without changing our beliefs we should move closer to other "christians" so that we can influence them for good. But though it would be quite right to want to encourage all those who profess a desire to follow God's way, we cannot do that by contradicting the commands of God. We cannot hope to please God by associating ourselves with other groups who do not believe the truth, no matter how joyful and sincere they may seem. It would be tantamount to going to Bethel to worship. Fellowship must be on the terms defined by God's Word. True disciples will forsake fellowship with false teachings in the churches and associate themselves with the ecclesia of Christ. Brethren and sisters who leave the ecclesia and join the churches are jumping into the lion's mouth. Josiah did not make that mistake.

5

"CASTING DOWN IMAGINATIONS"

WHEN Josiah was 16 years of age he began to seek the God of David his father. Just four years later he embarked upon a campaign to turn the nation back to the God he had found. "In the twelfth year (of his reign) he began to purge Judah and Jerusalem ..." (2 Chronicles 34:3). "Purge" means to cleanse, and there certainly was a huge job of cleaning up to do. The scale of the corruption can be appreciated from the fact that, even given the zeal with which he pursued the task, it took Josiah six years to complete it.

Cleansing the Land

Specifically mentioned in the Chronicles record are the "high places", "groves", "carved images", "molten images", "altars of Baalim" and "the images", all of which were instruments of idolatry. "The high places" refer to the open-air sanctuaries or churches of the pagan, built usually on a hill or mound, and used for the fertility cults of the Canaanite religions. It seems they would have an altar, a holy stele (a stone slab or pillar) and "the groves", which translates the Hebrew *asherim* and refers to the sacred trees and carvings which were placed in the ceremonial gardens associated with the "high places". They were used for ritual prostitution, including male prostitution. "Asherah" was the ancient mother goddess beloved of just about every civilisation of the area. In some myths she is the consort of Baal and both are associated with the power of fertility. The carnal rites of the worship confirm the appropriateness of the use of the term "whoredom" in Scripture to describe Israel's idolatry.

At one archaeological site, the high place at Gezer, investigations revealed a line of limestone pillars on a raised platform. There was also a large limestone block about 6 x 5 x 2 feet (1.8 x 1.5 x 0.6 m) in which was cut a square depression about 2 feet (0.6 m) deep.* It is thought probable that this was a socket for a pillar or carved image of wood representing Asherah. Manasseh had made such images, and Amon his son had worshipped them (2 Chronicles 33:22). (Further discussion of these objects, as well as discussion of the altars and images described in the 2 Kings 23 record is found in Chapter 10.)

But where had these abominations come from? We are told that after his conversion Manasseh took away the idols and images out of the land, including the altars he had positioned in Jerusalem. Yet here they were once more in use in the land. (Had they really ever been displaced from their central position in the hearts and minds of the people?) 2 Kings 23:12 makes reference to the altars which Manasseh had made: "And the altars ... did the king beat down ... and cast the dust of them into the brook Kidron." Somebody must have rescued these altars and kept them in store, then repositioned them after Manasseh's death. If such artefacts had been discovered in the modern era they would be treated as precious works of art to be displayed in the museums of the world. But in Jerusalem at that time they were displayed for worship not curiosity.

The Altars of Baalim

The Scripture record shows that Josiah personally supervised their destruction and indicates how zealously he undertook that work:

> "And they brake down the altars of Baalim in his presence; and the images, that were on high above them, he cut down; and the groves, and the carved images, and the molten images, he brake in pieces, and made dust of them, and strowed it upon the graves of them that had sacrificed unto them. And he burned the bones of the priests upon their altars, and cleansed Judah and Jerusalem." (2 Chronicles 34:4,5)

This was a complete destruction. He pulled down the idols, broke them apart and then pulverised them. Never again would they be used for worship. It could not have been an easy task. How did they grind the images to

---

* This is pictured in *The Lion Handbook to the Bible*, page 251 and *The Lion Photoguide to the Bible*, page 50.

powder? It probably took longer to do that than to make them in the first place! But it was what Moses had done at Sinai. At that time Moses "took the calf which they had made, and burnt it in the fire, and ground it to powder, and strawed it upon the water, and made the children of Israel drink of it" (Exodus 32:20).

And it was not just in Judah that Josiah carried out this work. His zeal was not bound by formal borders. He travelled through the territory of the former ten tribes as far as the region of Galilee: "So did he in the cities of Manasseh, and Ephraim, and Simeon, even unto Naphtali, with their mattocks round about" (2 Chronicles 34:6). "Mattocks" translates the ordinary Hebrew word for "sword". Here we have a picture of Josiah with his followers tearing through the land with a fury, with their swords flashing, scything down everything that was offensive to God. The description of their work outside Jerusalem in verse 7 is almost identical to that describing the earlier work in the city: "And when he had broken down the altars and the groves, and had beaten the graven images into powder, and cut down all the idols throughout all the land of Israel, he returned to Jerusalem."

Josiah's Inspiration?

What Josiah did to the idols was exactly what God had instructed Israel to do when they came into the promised land: "Ye shall destroy their altars, and brake down their images, and cut down their groves, and burn their graven images with fire" (Deuteronomy 7:5). But Josiah would not have known that. The book of Deuteronomy had not been rediscovered at that time. Where then did Josiah's inspiration come from? Was it from the records of the house of David? His forebear Asa had done something similar. He had destroyed the idol his mother had set up and "stamped (pulverised) it, and burnt it at the brook Kidron" (2 Chronicles 15:16). And it was what had been done under the reformation of Hezekiah: "All Israel that were present went out to the cities of Judah, and brake the images in pieces, and cut down the groves, and threw down the high places and the altars out of all Judah and Benjamin, in Ephraim also and Manasseh, until they had utterly destroyed them all" (2 Chronicles 31:1).

It seems to be the general rule that faithful kings of Judah took responsibility for the worship of the whole of the land of Israel as promised to Abraham, and not just of the two tribes which remained after the folly of Rehoboam. Asa and Hezekiah would have been powerful examples to Josiah.

A Second Cleansing Required!

Given the completeness of this work of Josiah it is very surprising to find that soon after he returned to Jerusalem he had to start work all over again. The chronology of events in the two records of Kings and Chronicles needs to be studied carefully, but it shows that in fact there were two separate cleansings of the land.

The first cleansing is that recorded in 2 Chronicles 34 and which we have examined above. That section ends with the words, "Now in the eighteenth year of his reign, when he had purged the land, and the house, he sent Shaphan ... to repair the house of the LORD his God" (verse 8). In other words, the first cleansing was completed before the temple restoration and the discovery of the Law.

The account in 2 Kings 22 does not refer to the first cleansing of the land. Detailed commentary begins in the eighteenth year of Josiah's reign. It records the response of Josiah to hearing the Word and the subsequent actions which he took. Those actions included instruction to Hilkiah to cleanse the temple of idols: "And the king commanded Hilkiah the high priest ... to bring forth out of the temple of the LORD all the vessels that were made for Baal, and for the grove, and for all the host of heaven" (2 Kings 23:4). There follows a more detailed account of the cleansing of not only the temple and the city but of the whole land. That this was indeed a second cleansing after the discovery of the Law is confirmed by the reference at the end of the account which says, "Moreover the workers with familiar spirits, and the wizards, and the images, and the idols, and all the abominations that were spied in the land of Judah and in Jerusalem, did Josiah put away, that he might perform the words of the law which were written in the book that Hilkiah the priest found in the house of the LORD" (verse 24).

If this analysis is correct it means that no sooner had Josiah left Jerusalem for the countryside than the authorities back in Jerusalem re-erected the images, as they had done after the death of Manasseh. Did they have to recast and re-carve the idols, or were they imported? Perhaps when they realised what Josiah was intent on doing, the priests hid some of their idols out of harm's way. What is clear is that there was no shortage of images to worship even though Josiah had done as much as was physically possible to destroy them. And the same must have been true outside Jerusalem, because those areas also had to be cleansed again.

The Remnant of Baal to be Destroyed

The surprising fact of two cleansings, with the implication that after the first at least some of the people had reconstructed the paraphernalia of apostasy, sheds light on the prophecy of Zephaniah. Zephaniah, a cousin of the king, prophesied during the reign of Josiah. Zephaniah's reference to idolatry in Jerusalem is usually taken to indicate that the prophecy was delivered early on in Josiah's reign, before he reached twenty years of age. But notice the careful description of the apostasy. Zephaniah chapter 1 says:

> "I will also stretch out mine hand upon Judah, and upon all the inhabitants of Jerusalem; and I will cut off the remnant of Baal from this place, and the name of the Chemarims with the priests; and them that worship the host of heaven upon the housetops; and them that worship and that swear by the LORD, and that swear by Malcham; and them that are turned back from the LORD; and those that have not sought the LORD, nor enquired for him." (verses 4-6)

Reference to the "remnant of Baal" suggests that an attempt to destroy Baal worship had already taken place but was not completely successful. This would fit with the view that the people were conspiring to preserve their pagan ways behind Josiah's back. The Chemarim are mentioned in the second cleansing in 2 Kings 23:5 where it says that "he put down the idolatrous priests (Chemarim)". The idea in the phrase "put down" is 'cause to cease', suggesting that Josiah would be the one who fulfilled Zephaniah's prophecy. The worshipping of the sun, moon and stars was practised, so Zephaniah says, on the rooftops. Was this because Josiah had already pulled down the high places and the images to the sun where the people used to worship the host of heaven? Verse 5 of Zephaniah 1 also suggests that there were those who made a gesture of worshipping Yahweh, but at the same time also worshipped Malcham the god of the Moabites: "Them that worship and swear by the LORD, and that swear by Malcham". Verse 6 refers to "them that are turned back from the LORD". All this is consistent with the dating of the prophecy between the two cleansings which Josiah carried out.

Zephaniah continues to denounce the wickedness of Jerusalem and describes impending judgement. He says, "And it shall come to pass at that time, that I will search Jerusalem with candles, and will punish the men that are settled on their lees: that say in their heart, The LORD will not do good, neither will he do evil" (1:12). Is this a reference to the secret practices of the idolaters, who hid from the reforms of Josiah? Zephaniah shows that they did not believe in Yahweh; their hearts were elsewhere and they were biding their time until the storm of Josiah's reformation was past. During the second, and apparently even more thorough cleansing, Josiah sought out all the remnant of Baal: "All the abominations that were spied in the land of Judah and in Jerusalem did Josiah put away" (2 Kings 23:24). Included in this were the teraphim, the small house gods. Did Josiah literally take a lamp and search from house to house for those idols? Those that could not be seen by Josiah were known to God, and the coming judgement on the last generation would remove them all.

Josiah Foreshadowed Christ

There are some powerful lessons in these events, lessons which are reinforced by the fact that the events set a pattern which the Lord Jesus himself followed. In Scripture there are two records of the cleansing of the temple by the Master. As is the case for Josiah's work, close comparison shows that these were on two different occasions.

41

The first is recorded in John 2 when the Lord overturned the tables of the money changers and drove out the animals. The incident made the disciples recall the words of Psalm 69: "The zeal of thine house hath eaten me up." Three years later it was just the same when the Lord went into the temple and looked around; his earlier actions and subsequent teachings had made no difference to their thinking at all. A second time he overturned the tables of the money-changers and drove out the animals from his Father's house. The rulers challenged his actions with the question, "By what authority doest thou these things? and who gave thee this authority?" (Matthew 21:23). Had they recognised the similarity between the Lord's act and the purging of the temple by Josiah? The authority was that of the King, the Lord's anointed.

Idolatry Today

The "idols" which the Master had to deal with in the temple were those to do with the idolatry of covetousness (Colossians 3:5) and the love of mammon. Religion for the ruling class was a means of personal gain. It was the religion which Jeroboam would have immediately recognised – the sort of religion which the Apostle Paul denounces in 1 Timothy 6. This sort of idolatry is a grave threat to our salvation as well. The apostle says in Ephesians 5:5, "For this ye know, that no whoremonger, nor unclean person, nor covetous man, who is an idolater, hath any inheritance in the kingdom of Christ and of God".

We need to think carefully about this modern form of idolatry, especially as most of us live in an affluent world where time and opportunity are plentiful. In the last days of the generation of Josiah's children Ezekiel exposed the roots of idolatry. In chapter 8 of his prophecy he is given a vision of the temple at Jerusalem whose inner walls were painted with idolatrous images. "Then said he unto me, Son of man, hast thou seen what the ancients of the house of Israel do in the dark, every man in the chambers of his imagery? for they say, The LORD seeth us not; for the LORD hath forsaken the earth" (verse 12). The word for "imagery" (*maskiyth*) indicates a picture. In chapter 14 the Lord declares to Ezekiel, "Son of man, these men have set

42

up their idols in their heart" (verse 3). The chamber of the temple was but the outward expression of the chamber of their minds in which their imaginations had painted the images of idolatry.

Images – and the Imagination

This exposé of idolatry in Ezekiel 14 is based in turn upon Leviticus 26. There are numerous references in Ezekiel 14 to the warnings against idolatry in Leviticus 26. Leviticus 26:1 is a key verse. Close examination reveals a sequence of thought which illuminates the process of idolatry. The verse says, "Ye shall make you no idols nor graven image, neither rear you up a standing image, neither shall ye set up any image of stone in your land, to bow down unto it: for I am the LORD your God". The first word translated "idols" (*eliyl*) has the sense of 'good for nothing'. The next in order is the "graven image", a carving or a sculpture by which the worthless thought is converted into a tangible and visible form. After this comes the rearing up of a "standing image" or pillar. The worthless thought has not only been given shape but it has now been set up to attract attention and stimulate the imagination. The final step in the development of idolatry is represented by the setting up of the "image of stone". The word "image" (*maskiyth*) is the word for picture, the first occurrence of this word in Scripture. The idol has now been given detail and colour and commands the attention and time of its devotees.

Is not this a serious danger in our own lives? We start with a thought or desire which arises from our natural impulses. If we were to expose it to the light of scriptural scrutiny straight away we would see that it is not in harmony with the things of God and is therefore good for nothing and to be rejected. But by not rejecting it, by holding it in the mind, the imagination can work on it. First of all it gives substance to the idea which can then be remembered and called to mind during idle moments. If we are not careful it becomes the predominant thought which we turn over and over in our minds, as a craftsman might turn the wood on the lathe. The result is that the idol is beginning to take detailed shape and beginning to displace other things from our mind. Our imaginations can easily work through the consequences of the thought, developing our anticipation of fulfilling the desire, embellishing the detail, and making it into a vividly colourful object which we crave. Then we are tempted to direct our lives to attain that object. We have been seduced into the worship of an idol!

Grinding Idols to Powder

The right way to deal with idols is demonstrated by Josiah. He ground them to powder. It is no good us merely shifting them out of central focus. Human nature is such that when the opportunity comes we will put them right back. We have to deal with our idols ruthlessly: "If thine eye offend thee, pluck it out." This is what is going to happen anyway when the kingdom of men and all that is associated with it is destroyed by the stone power of the Kingdom of God as described in Daniel 2. Far better for us to deal the death blow to idolatry in our lives now than share the fate of the image of the kingdom of men, when Christ returns.

For this is what the Lord Jesus said would happen to those who refused to recognise his supreme authority over their lives. Immediately after he had cleansed the temple and the leaders had challenged his authority, he replied with a stern warning in the parable of the husbandmen. That parable, which shows the authority of the Lord as the Son of God, concludes with the explanation: "Therefore say I unto you, the kingdom of God shall be taken from you, and given to a nation bringing forth the fruits thereof. And whosoever shall fall on this stone shall be broken: but on whomsoever it shall fall, it will grind him to powder" (Matthew 21:43,44).

6

REPAIRING THE HOUSE OF GOD

"Now in the eighteenth year of his reign, when he had purged the land, and the house, he sent Shaphan the son of Azaliah, and Maaseiah the governor of the city, and Joah the son of Joahaz the recorder, to repair the house of the LORD his God."   (2 Chronicles 34:8)

AFTER Josiah had finished his first cleansing of the land, he returned to Jerusalem and set about repairing the temple. The decision which Josiah took immediately after he had returned from destroying the idols in the land to repair (more literally, to strengthen) the house of God shows that he was as concerned to emphasise the positive things which should fill it as he was to remove the abominations. And Josiah made it possible for all the people to be involved in this work, even those in the northern territories who might have been considered unworthy of participating.

He sent three of his servants, Shaphan, Maaseiah and Joah, to Hilkiah the high priest. 2 Chronicles 34 says that they "delivered the money that was brought into the house of God, which the Levites that kept the doors had gathered of the hand of Manasseh and Ephraim, and of all the remnant of Israel, and of all Judah and Benjamin" (verse 9; 2 Kings 22:4). This suggests that either the remnant of the northern tribes had been encouraged to come to Jerusalem to worship and to make their contribution, or that during his journey through their land Josiah had collected donations for the work of repair which were then added to the collections taken up at the door of the temple.

This approach of emphasising the positive things of the Truth, even in a time of depressing faithlessness, is in keeping with the spirit of the Master's parable in which he warns of the dangers of creating a spiritual vacuum in our lives:

"When the unclean spirit is gone out of a man, he walketh through dry places, seeking rest; and finding none, he saith, I will return unto my house whence I came out. And when he cometh, he findeth it swept and garnished. Then goeth he, and taketh to him seven other spirits more wicked than himself ... and the last state of that man is worse than the first."

(Luke 11:24-26)

This was the case with the Pharisees who would have avoided any hint of idolatry in formal worship and yet were themselves thoroughly corrupted within their hearts. Their tradition which was to "perish with the using" was characterised by ordinances of "touch not; taste not; handle not" (Colossians 2:21). The counter to this way of thinking was summarised by the apostle: "Put off all these ... put on the new man ... put on therefore, as the elect of God, holy and beloved, bowels of mercies ..." (3:8-12).

A Positive Approach

Too easily we can concentrate upon the negative and not take time to put something positive in its place. The space created in our thoughts by removing the idols of covetousness must be filled with the positive things of Bible study, prayer and meditation on the Word. In ecclesial life too the removal of problem situations must be followed up by creating wholesome, positive activity for fellowship and preaching. We should beware of developing a carping and critical attitude which can see no spiritual profit in any activity unless it is completely flawless. Doctrinal problems must be tackled but we must be sure to substitute positive, wholesome and lively Bible study. (Is it not the case that an ecclesia which is busy preaching the Truth is much less likely to get serious doctrinal problems to deal with from within?) Apathy towards the Word gives unsound speculations the space to grow into problems. We must deal with wayward young people in the ecclesia and the difficult situations which sometimes arise, but then we must provide sound, wholesome and enjoyable activities to draw out and encourage their better qualities.

46

Constant carping on negatives can only depress the enthusiasm of those who are sound, and crush any budding interest the weak may have. If Josiah had adopted that attitude there would have been no reformation at all, merely an iconoclastic fury followed by a trail of dust in his wake. Instead he worked in the ruins of the house of God to build up a community in which at least some maintained a faithful witness, and laid the foundation for restoration after the seventy years captivity. He did it, because, as it says in 2 Chronicles 34:8, it was the house of "the LORD his God". He had originally sought the God "of David his father", but now the Lord had become his God. The work of repair was not a political tactic to strengthen the kingdom, it was an act of devotion and love towards his God.

The same was true on a greater level in the work of the Lord Jesus Christ. He so rightly denounced the hypocrisy of the scribes and Pharisees and pronounced the impending destruction of their temple: "Behold, your house is left unto you desolate" (Matthew 23:38); "There shall not be left one stone upon another, that shall not be thrown down" (Mark 13:2). But his work was to repair the house of God: "For the Son of man is as a man taking a far journey, who left his house, and gave authority to his servants, and to every man his work, and commanded the porter to watch. Watch ye therefore: for ye know not when the master (Lord) of the house cometh" (verses 34,35). Despite the tribulations which were to come upon the nation, the reassurance which he gave to his disciples was: "In my Father's house are many abiding places ... I go to prepare a place for you. And ... I will come again, and receive you unto myself; that where I am, there ye may be also" (John 14:2,3).

A Spiritual Work

Three groups of workers can be identified: the overseers, the skilled craftsmen and the labourers. The money for the temple repairs was given to the "workmen that had the oversight of the house of the LORD, and they gave it to the workmen that wrought in the house of the LORD" (2 Chronicles 34:10). Also mentioned in 2 Chronicles 34:13 are "the bearers of burdens". It would be invidious to try

47

to specify equivalent rôles today within the organisation of ecclesias. The skills required to build up the house of God are not so simply identified. Skilful building and craftsmanship will be operating at all sorts of levels: for example, it may be found in the kindly wisdom of an older sister who counsels a younger sister and prevents a family problem developing. It may be there in the quiet reassuring character of a brother or sister which encourages young people to confide in them. In these more delicate areas of building many of us can be but fetchers and carriers for those who have developed the skills of the spiritual artisan. But that is not to be decried, for the work of strengthening the house of God involves all of us.

The money that had been collected was to be given to buy "timber and hewn stone to repair the house" (2 Kings 22:6). The impression we are given is of extensive damage to the house having taken place in the reigns of Manasseh and Amon and which was now to be remedied. The Chronicles record refers not just to the need to repair the house but also to the need to "amend (fasten) the house". Was the house in such a state of dereliction that it was falling down? There is also reference to "timber for couplings, and to floor (or rafter) the houses which the kings of Judah had destroyed" (2 Chronicles 34:11).

What a terrible indictment on the kings of Judah! How great an effort David had made at the end of his life to prepare the materials to build the house of the Lord. David had said to Solomon: "The house ... must be exceeding magnifical, of fame and of glory throughout all countries" (1 Chronicles 22:5). Yet David's descendants had looted and polluted and then neglected their most important responsibility so that its basic structure was unsound. It is worth noting here that apostasy is not merely adding that which is false to the heritage we have been given, but it also involves breaking down the true. When the false is removed we must be sure to rebuild the understanding of the first principles of the Truth, and not assume that the structure is sound. For Josiah the work of pulling down the trappings of apostasy may not have seemed such hard work compared to the effort required to build up the house of the Lord! Yet he was following the best example.

The men in charge were "Jahath and Obadiah, the Levites, of the sons of Merari; and Zechariah and Meshullam, of the sons of the Kohathites" (2 Chronicles 34:12). The Levitical role in this most practical activity is emphasised in the repeated phrase of 2 Kings 22:5: "And let them deliver (the money) into the hand of the doers of the work, that have the oversight of the house of the LORD ... to repair the breaches of the house." The "doers of the work" was one of the descriptions of the Levites when they were given their commission by Moses. They were enrolled, "From thirty years old and upward even until fifty years old, all that enter into the host, to do the work in the tabernacle of the congregation" (Numbers 4:3). The work of the Levites, as doers of the Word, was at the same time both spiritual and practical. They ministered to the priests in fetching and carrying so that fellowship with the God of Israel could be made accessible to the nation. The Apostle Paul, who in his epistles exhorted Timothy to see himself as a spiritual Levite in the service of the High Priest, says: "But watch thou in all things, endure afflictions, do the work of an evangelist, make full proof of thy ministry" (2 Timothy 4:5).* He was speaking about the responsibility which Timothy had to counter false teachings in the ecclesia but then also to build up the house of God.

Workmen that need not be ashamed
The Levites in turn gave the money for the repairs to the "artificers", that is, to the masons, carpenters, builders and so on. Other skilled craftsmen in Jerusalem in that last generation are mentioned by Jeremiah as using their skills to fabricate idols: "For the customs of the people are vain: for one cutteth a tree out of the forest, the work of the hands of the workman, with the axe. They deck it with silver and with gold ... the work of the workman, and of the hands of the founder ... they are all the work of cunning men" (Jeremiah 10:3,4,9). The lesson here is that

* Compare 1 Timothy 1:18 with Numbers 4:23, AV margin.

the same God-given skills which should be used to build up His house can also be squandered on self.

In contrast to the craftsmen who wasted their talents on idols, Jeremiah goes on to describe craftsmen who were blessed under the providential care of God. Amongst those who are listed as going into captivity in Babylon with Jeconiah were "the carpenters and smiths" (Jeremiah 24:1). This event was just 24 years after the beginning of the repair of the temple, and therefore the craftsmen concerned would almost certainly have included some who had been part of Josiah's reformation. They were taken into captivity, not as a punishment; on the contrary, as a safeguard, because they were faithful. Those who were taken into captivity were explained to Jeremiah as the "good figs", that is, people who brought forth fruit unto God. Of these the Lord says:

"Like these good figs, so will I acknowledge them that are carried away captive of Judah, whom I have sent out of the place into the land of the Chaldeans for their good. For I will set mine eyes upon them for good, and I will bring them again to this land: and I will build them, and not pull them down; and I will plant them, and not pluck them up." (Jeremiah 24:5,6)

The craftsmen of Jerusalem who were associated with strengthening the house of God can therefore be seen to represent the disciples of Christ who faithfully endeavour to upbuild the ecclesia and who find a place in the Kingdom of God.

The promise which the Lord makes to the craftsmen of Jerusalem is part of a rich theme in Scripture. It brings together the idea of the house and the field. The work is both to do with a building – "I will build them", and a plant – "I will plant them". The theme can be traced right back to the time when Israel were taken out of Egypt. The Song of Moses describes the aim of their deliverance in these terms: "Thou shalt bring them in, and plant them in the mountain of thine inheritance, in the place, O LORD, which thou hast made for thee to dwell in, in the Sanctuary, O LORD, which thy hands have established" (Exodus 15:17). When David ascended to the throne he wanted to build God a house, but the answer that came back repeated the Lord's original aim: "Also I will ordain a place for my people Israel, and will plant them, and they shall dwell in their place, and shall be moved no more ... Furthermore I tell thee that the LORD will build thee an house" (1 Chronicles 17:9,10).

The Apostle Paul summarises the theme when he says to the Corinthians:

"I have planted, Apollos watered; but God gave the increase. So then neither is he that planteth any thing, neither he that watereth; but God that giveth the increase. Now he that planteth and he that watereth are one: and every man shall receive his own reward according to his own labour. For we are labourers together with God: ye are God's husbandry, ye are God's building." (1 Corinthians 3:6-10)

In these metaphors the strength and stability of the stone building is combined with the vitality and fruitfulness of the plant to describe the ecclesia of Christ. The same idea can be traced in other places, including Colossians 2:6,7: "As ye have therefore received Christ Jesus the Lord, so walk ye in him: rooted (as a plant) and built up in him, and stablished (as a building) in the faith, as ye have been taught, abounding (as a plant) therein with thanksgiving."

Jeremiah 24 also draws out a spiritual paradox. The builders of the house of God themselves become the building – "I will build them, and not pull them down"! The building which is being constructed, the house of God, is always the work of His hands, even though we are called upon to use all the skills which the Lord has given us in the work. In Exodus 15 the house which was to be built is called "the Sanctuary, O LORD, which thy hands have established". When David wanted to build the Lord a house he was told: "I will build thee an house." The growth of the building comes through God and we, at best, are tools in His hand. In apostolic times the house of God was to be "builded together for an habitation of God through the Spirit" (Ephesians 2:22), the individual stones of the building being the workers themselves: "Ye also, as lively stones, are built up a spiritual house, an holy priesthood" (1 Peter 2:5).

Working in Faithfulness

The character of those engaged in repairing the house of God under the reforms of Josiah is worthy of note. The Scriptures record this tribute to the honesty of the workmen: "Howbeit there was no reckoning made with them of the money that was delivered into their hand, because they dealt faithfully" (2 Kings 22:7). A more literal rendering says, "in faithfulness they are dealing" (Interlinear Bible). The Chronicles record says: "The men did the work faithfully" (2 Chronicles 34:12). The same was true at the time of the repairs to the house in the reign of Jehoash: "Moreover they reckoned not with the men, into whose hand they delivered the money to be bestowed on workmen: for they dealt faithfully" (2 Kings 12:15). Faithfulness inspires trust, which in turn increases the commitment of those trusted and the sense of fellowship in the work of the Lord, and brings out the best in the servants of God. The faithfulness of the workers explains why they were to be blessed in the way described in Jeremiah 24, as the Proverbs say: "A faithful man shall abound with blessings" (28:20).

The same spiritual qualities of faithfulness and honesty are required of God's servants in all ages: "It is required in stewards, that a man be found faithful" (1 Corinthians 4:2); and in all their activities: "He that is faithful in that which is least is faithful also in much" (Luke 16:10). Honesty is demanded in business, and not just because we are under scrutiny from our bosses and may be caught out, with all the embarrassment which that would entail, but for higher motives: "Not with eyeservice, as menpleasers; but in singleness of heart, fearing God: and whatsoever ye do, do it heartily, as to the Lord, and not unto men" (Colossians 3:22,23). The work of the Truth must in the same way be conducted by people of integrity who can be trusted to deal faithfully. Paul commanded Timothy: "And the things that thou hast heard of me among many witnesses, the same commit thou to faithful men, who shall be able to teach others also" (2 Timothy 2:2).

It is incumbent on brethren in all their teaching to be faithful to the Word of God if they are to build up the household of faith. Speculations and hypotheses, usually drawn from writers who do not reverence the Scriptures as the Word of God, may have intellectual appeal but they have no place in the house of God. And the principle also applies to personal relationships within the ecclesia. The Apostle John commends an ecclesia with the words, "Beloved, thou doest faithfully whatsoever thou doest to the brethren, and to strangers" (3 John 5).

Working in Harmony

The third class of workers engaged in the temple repairs, the labourers, were under the supervision of a very unexpected group of Levites. The point is made again more clearly in the RSV translation of 2 Chronicles 34:12,13: "The Levites, all who were skilful with instruments of music, were over the burden bearers and directed all who did work in every kind of service; and some of the Levites were scribes, and officials, and gatekeepers." Levites skilled in orchestrating the worship of the temple were to use that ability to harmonise the contributions which the labourers were making.

Here is another link with the ecclesia of Christ. When Paul writes to the Corinthians about true fellowship in Christ he asks: "And what concord hath Christ with Belial? or what part hath he that believeth with an infidel? And what agreement hath the temple of God with idols? for ye are the temple of the living God" (2 Corinthians 6:15,16). In this passage the word translated "concord" is *sumphonesis* from which our 'symphony' is derived. Its cognate word *sumphonia* is translated as "music" in Luke 15:25. The sense of the word is of agreement between the different instruments; not of course meaning that each must give the same note, but that each participant taking direction from the leader, contributes harmoniously to the one piece. This describes ecclesial life as it should be, working in harmony together to edify one another in love.

7

DISCOVERING THE WORD OF GOD

W E can see Josiah's positive approach to the things of the Truth even when he was engaged in destroying those things which were contrary to the Truth. Already under way during the period of cleansing the land was the collection of funds to finance the repairs to the house. When Josiah returned to Jerusalem he gave instructions about the use of those funds. And it was when the money was being taken out of the treasury in the house of the Lord that the most significant event in the whole of Josiah's reign occurred, the pivotal point in the history of that generation and which had profound effects on the future of the nation – the discovery of the Law of the Lord.

The Word of God was Lost!

To understand the significance of the event we need to appreciate that the Law must have been lost for some considerable time. That is, not only had the temple copy been mislaid but there were no copies available to the king or the rulers until that discovery by Hilkiah. This becomes clear when we see Josiah's reaction to the reading of the Law by Shaphan. He was devastated: "And it came to pass, when the king had heard the words of the book of the law, that he rent his clothes" (2 Kings 22:11). The prophetess Huldah indicates that not only did Josiah tear his clothes but he also wept when he heard the words (2 Chronicles 34:27). We can conclude from this that despite seeking the God of David for the previous ten years, this was the first time he had heard the Law. If there had been another copy in the land at that time, then six years travelling through the countryside pulling down idols and seeking the lost sheep of the house of Israel had not revealed it. Even the priests did not have their own copy. Jeremiah the son of the High Priest exclaimed at the discovery: "Thy words were found, and I did eat them; and thy word was unto me the joy and rejoicing of mine heart" (Jeremiah 15:16).

The fact that the Law had been "lost" is an extraordinary thought. This was not carelessness! It was the most telling barometer of the decline of the nation of Judah. Perhaps in the days of Manasseh the Word of God had been hunted down and destroyed – as thoroughly as Josiah was now hunting down idolatry. Some Scriptures must have been available to Josiah in order to enable him to discover the God of David he was seeking. But there were traps and pitfalls and Josiah would have had to be cautious. This is clear from the words of Jeremiah in the early part of his prophecy, probably before the discovery of the Law. He rebuked the scribes with the words: "How do ye say, We are wise, and the law of the LORD is with us? Lo, certainly in vain made he it; the pen of the scribes is in vain ('the false pen of the scribes worketh for falsehood', AV margin). The wise men are ashamed, they are dismayed and taken: lo, they have rejected the word of the LORD; and what wisdom is in them?" (Jeremiah 8:8,9).

The scribes were making claims to have the Word of the Lord but had been caught out – they were "ashamed". Was this the result of the discovery of the Law? Were they making false claims for their own writings, or were they making "copies" of Scripture which deliberately falsified the text? There can be no more serious deception than that. If those who were charged with the responsibility to safeguard the Word handled it deceitfully, how could the common people hear God's message? We may surmise with some probability that in their false copies the judgements of God against Israel had been omitted, for it was these judgements which Josiah heard for the first time through the discovery of Hilkiah. The message the false prophets liked to give was, "Peace, peace; when there is no peace" (Jeremiah 8:11).

There is a modern day equivalent of the deception of the scribes in the days of Jeremiah – doctrinally biased translations and paraphrases of the Bible or sections of it which falsify the teaching of the original texts. For example, *The Living Bible* of John 1 says, "Before anything else existed, there was Christ, with God". The *Good News Bible* says that Jesus Christ "always had the nature of God" (Philippians 2:6). The NIV of the same passage says, "being in very nature God". The Greek text says no such thing, using the word "form" and not "nature".* Another example is the false doctrine of heaven-going which is implied by the *Good News Bible* in Philippians 3:14, "... the prize, which is God's call through Christ Jesus to the life above", and similarly in the NIV, "... the prize for which God has called me heavenwards in Christ Jesus". The existence of such "translations" makes discussion and debate with our critics more difficult. When we have to explain that the original text says something different from what they read in their "Bibles" it may seem to be special pleading. "The odd mistranslation may be forgiven, but when there is a frequent obscuring of vital truth, and sometimes blatant distortion of that truth, one must ponder the wisdom of using such a translation."**

Look for it then!

The loss of the Scriptures explains a very pointed comment of Jeremiah in chapter 2:31: "O generation, see ye the word of the LORD." We are well used to the expression to do with hearing the Word of the Lord, but "see the Word" is a unique phrase in Scripture. Would the people who heard Jeremiah understand the significance of these words? Was the loss of the Book something which was felt by the people? Or did they need to be exhorted even to consider the fact that it had been lost?

The discovery of the Law was the perfect answer to the academic deceptions of the scribes; the copy found was the original, in Moses' own handwriting. This is indicated in the text where the discovery by Hilkiah was said to be a book of the Law "by the hand of Moses" (2 Chronicles 34:14, margin). This in itself suggests it was the original, but the fact that Hilkiah seemed unable to read it for himself bears out the conclusion. "Hilkiah the high priest said unto Shaphan the scribe, I have found the book of the

---

* See Brother N. Mullen, "Philippians 2:6-11 – A Study in History and Exposition", *The Testimony*, 1985, pages 201-205.
** Brother K. White, *The Testimony*, May 1994, pages 150-154.

law in the house of the LORD. And Hilkiah gave the book to Shaphan, and he read it" (2 Kings 22:8). The ancient script which Moses would have used would have been unfamiliar to those not expert in writing, as Shaphan the scribe would have been. Here was the answer to the questions and controversies about the authenticity of what the scribes were claiming as the Word of God. In that respect it would have been comparable to the discovery in our own time of the Dead Sea Scrolls which confirm the accuracy of the copies which have come down to us by the providence of God. But of course in Josiah's day all true copies had been destroyed.

But what precisely was discovered? Which book of the Law? It is clear both from the context of the discovery and the way in which it is quoted by Jeremiah and Josiah that the main subject of interest was the book of Deuteronomy. Deuteronomy 31 records how the book came to be written: "And it came to pass, when Moses had made an end of writing the words of this law in a book, until they were finished, that Moses commanded the Levites, which bare the ark of the covenant of the LORD, saying, Take this book of the law, and put it in the side of the ark of the covenant of the LORD your God, that it may be there for a witness against thee" (verses 24-26). In later Scripture the expression "book of the law" is used a number of times, and wherever it can be determined precisely the references are to the book of Deuteronomy. Joshua, when he built the altar on Mount Ebal, fulfilled Deuteronomy 27:5,6 – "as it is written in the book of the law of Moses" (Joshua 8:31). "Afterward he read all the words of the law, the blessings and cursings, according to all that is written in the book of the law" (verse 34). Again it is Deuteronomy which is being referred to, this time chapter 28. 2 Kings 14:6 is directing attention to Deuteronomy 24:16 in the "book of the law". In the only occurrence of the phrase in the New Testament, in Galatians 3:10, the Apostle Paul is quoting from Deuteronomy 27:26.

All these references confirm the belief that the book discovered was Deuteronomy. But could it have been more than this? There is a hint in Joshua 24 that Deuteronomy was but the last section of a continuing record of God's

Word. "So Joshua made a covenant with the people that day, and set them a statute and an ordinance in Shechem. And Joshua wrote these words in the book of the law of God ..." (verses 25,26). If this book was the same one mentioned in chapter 8 then it seems that Joshua was adding "his" book to the canon of Scripture. The books of Genesis, Exodus, Leviticus and Numbers must have been recorded at some time during Moses' leadership and would need to be kept in a secure place. Where better than in the side of the ark where they would remain as a witness and as a reference work for future copyists?

A Treasure not to be Mislaid!

The fact that this book, written by Moses, had been lost was witness enough to the generation of Josiah and his children. And there is a special irony in the location where it was found. It had been separated from the ark (at the time of the temple repairs the ark was not in the temple – 2 Chronicles 35:3), but the book was still in the temple, in the treasury. It was "when they brought out the money that was brought into the house of the LORD, (that) Hilkiah the priest found" the book (2 Chronicles 34:14).

There is an important exhortation for us here. Even today the Word of God can be lost in the "house of God", the ecclesia, which is intended to be "the pillar and stay of the truth". This can happen if men's words replace God's Word as the basis for exhortation, if Bible study is not conducted faithfully and so the Word is not "rightly divided", and if preachers fail to expound "all the counsel of God". The cumulative effect over time of a diet of words which fails to capture the power of God's Word is bound to be spiritual lethargy and a falling away from the Truth. We should also take care that the Word is not lost in the "treasury", which can happen today if the material concerns of running ecclesial activities displace a proper emphasis upon the Word and replace the true spirit of Christ which is seen in kindness, thoughtfulness and consideration of the needs and feelings of all, but especially of the weak. Furthermore, the Word of God can be lost in our own homes when the daily round of life becomes so cluttered with business, social activities and entertainment that we forget – or do not find time – to do the readings and teach the children from the Word.

Discovering the "Word made flesh"!

In the ministry of the Lord Jesus there was a parallel to the events concerning the discovery of the Word of God in the treasury in the reign of Josiah. In the last week of the Master's ministry, the Lord Jesus had just cleansed the temple for the second time, in the spirit of Josiah's reformation. He had drawn attention to the lessons from Josiah's generation by quoting Jeremiah 7. That chapter was a denunciation of the attitude of the people towards the temple. They took great pride in its status in Jerusalem and used it for regular worship. But this was sheer hypocrisy. In their private lives they oppressed the stranger, fatherless and widow (verse 6); stole, committed adultery and swore falsely (verse 9). Through Jeremiah the Lord asks, "Is this house, which is called by my name, become a den of robbers in your eyes?" (verse 11). The Lord Jesus took hold of these words when he drove out those that bought and sold in the temple: "And he taught, saying unto them, Is it not written, My house shall be called of all nations the house of prayer? but ye have made it a den of thieves" (Mark 11:17).

There, in the temple, the Word of God was far from their thoughts. The Lord goes on to narrate parables, which we hope to show later were in part at least based upon the Scriptures of Josiah's time. As his opponents queued up to try to catch him out in argument the Lord challenged his critics with the words, "And have ye not read this scripture?" (Mark 12:10), and, "Do ye not therefore err, because ye know not the scriptures, neither the power of God?" (verse 24). He then confounded them by asking them to explain a verse in what must have been a very well known Psalm: "How say the scribes that Christ is the Son of David? For David himself said by the Holy Spirit, The LORD said to my Lord, Sit thou on my right hand, till I make thine enemies thy footstool" (verses 35,36).

In two senses the Word of God was lost in those days. It was missing from the understanding and the teaching of the scribes and Pharisees. Sometimes it is suggested that the problem with the scribes and Pharisees was that they had an undue regard for the Old Testament Scriptures and failed to see the new teaching of Jesus. This view misses the point the Lord was making. On another occasion he made the truth of the matter very clear when he applied the words of Isaiah's prophecy to them: "This people honoureth me with their lips, but their heart is far from me. Howbeit in vain do they worship me, teaching for doctrines the commandments of men" (Mark 7:6,7). They had rejected the Word of God to keep their own tradition.

But in another and even more significant way the Word of God was lost to them. The Word made flesh was there amongst them and the signs and wonders which he performed, and the gracious words which poured from his lips, were ample proof of who he was. But they could not find it in themselves to accept him.

The connection with Josiah's day grew stronger when in the temple a scribe approached and asked the Lord to say which was the greatest commandment in the Law. The answer Jesus gave was from the book of Deuteronomy: "The first of all the commandments is, Hear, O Israel; the Lord our God is one Lord: and thou shalt love the Lord thy God with all thy heart, and with all thy soul, and with all thy mind, and with all thy strength: this is the first commandment. And the second is like, namely this, Thou shalt love thy neighbour as thyself. There is none other commandment greater than these" (Mark 12:29-31). The scribe recognised that this answer was true and captured the very spirit of the law: "Well, Master, thou hast said the truth: for there is one God; and there is none other but he: and to love him with all the heart, and with all the understanding, and with all the soul, and with all the strength, and to love his neighbour as himself, is more than all whole burnt offerings and sacrifices" (Mark 11:32,33).

"With all his heart"

The response given by the scribe must have been no little encouragement to the Master: "When Jesus saw that he answered discreetly, he said unto him, Thou art not far from the kingdom of God" (verse 34). Despite all the depressing similarities between the spiritual state of the nation during the Lord's ministry and the reign of Josiah, here at least was one man who understood what Josiah was about. To Josiah the Word of God was not an ancient text to be criticised and "corrected" and added to, as was the case with the scribes of Jeremiah's day and the Lord's, but it was the living Word of God at which he trembled. The Word was to be believed and followed out of a love for the One who had revealed it. The testimony of God to the spirit of Josiah's life emphasises this: "And like unto him was there no king before him, that turned to the LORD with all his heart, and with all his soul, and with all his might, according to all the law of Moses" (2 Kings 23:25). Josiah is the only person in Scripture who is described as responding to the Lord in this way, with all his heart, soul and mind. But could not the scribe see that there before him in the temple, with all the authority of the King, was a greater even than Josiah, the perfect embodiment of the Law of love?

The Mark record goes on immediately to record an incident which demonstrated the principles just expounded but now seen in action in a very striking way. "Jesus sat over against the treasury, and beheld how the people cast money into the treasury." In Josiah's day the collection coffers had been set out for just the same purpose. He saw a widow putting into the treasury collection one farthing. In those days widows were poor partly because of rich men, some of whom grew richer because they devoured "widows' houses" (verse 40). They put in more than she had in monetary terms, but their contribution was of infinitesimal value in God's sight. Jesus called his disciples to see. He said: "This poor widow hath cast more in, than all they which have cast into the treasury: for all they did cast in of their abundance; but she of her want did cast in all that she had, even all her living" (verses 43,44).

"All that she had"

The emphasis in the Mark account, adding "all that she had", and stressing with repetition the word "all", links this incident to Deuteronomy 6:4 which Jesus had just quoted. Here was in truth an example of loving the Lord God with "all". The widow had had a choice to make. The record says that "she threw in two mites, which make a

61

farthing" (Mark 11:42). She had two coins and could have put in half of all she had. That would in comparative terms still have dwarfed the contribution of the rich. But she put both coins in, *"all* that she had". The Word of God had not been lost in her life. There in the treasury amidst an evil and adulterous generation could be found the Word of God as a power in the devotion of that widow. She stands in the record an an exhortation to us all of the need to translate the Word of God into the practicalities of daily life. The widow also shows that the fulfilment of the spirit of the Law is within the possibilities of all. "For if there be first a willing mind, it is accepted according to that a man hath, and not according to that he hath not" (2 Corinthians 8:12).

The giving of "all" is not of course to do principally with ecclesial collections! It represents the meaning of the burnt offering under the Law, as recognised by the scribe who questioned Jesus. Each one of us is asked to give ourselves wholeheartedly to the service of God in the way Josiah did: "By him therefore let us offer the sacrifice of praise to God continually, that is, the fruit of our lips giving thanks to his name. But to do good and to communicate forget not: for with such sacrifices God is well pleased" (Hebrews 13:15,16).

8

PERSONAL DISCOVERY OF THE WORD
IS ESSENTIAL

THE discovery of the lost book of the Law by Hilkiah in the treasury of the house of the Lord was the most significant event in the reign of Josiah. It had a profound effect upon the Godly king and a lasting effect upon a group of young people who were taken captive into Babylon, there to nurture a faith which would enable many to return from Babylon back to Jerusalem.

"A book" or "the book"?

Shaphan the scribe was able to read the ancient script in Moses' handwriting, but it is not clear that he understood the significance of the find. We are told that "Shaphan carried the book to the king, and brought the king word back again, saying, All that was committed to thy servants, they do it. And they have gathered together the money that was found in the house of the LORD, and have delivered it into the hand of the overseers, and to the hand of the workmen. Then Shaphan the scribe told the king, saying, Hilkiah the priest hath given me a book" (2 Chronicles 34:16-18). There is no hint here of the breathless excitement we imagine would have gripped Jeremiah after reading the scroll. Shaphan first delivers his report of the business in hand and only at the end mentions the book, and even then it is "a book", not "the book of the Law" which Hilkiah had clearly understood it to be.

What a different response Josiah showed. He understood immediately the enormity of the discovery and the significance of its content. Josiah refers more than once to "the words of this book" which had such impact upon his thinking. First of all he says, "Go ye, enquire of the LORD for me, and for the people, and for all Judah, concerning the words of this book that is found" (2 Kings 22:13). The message of the book was not just for the king, it was not a royal privilege in that sense, it was for everyone. And the reason was that they all were in the same desperate position: "For great is the wrath of the LORD that is kindled against us, because our fathers have not hearkened unto the words of this book, to do according unto all that which is written concerning us" (verse 13). The reply through Huldah picks up this emphasis in the thinking of Josiah: "Tell the man that sent you to me, Thus saith the LORD, Behold, I will bring evil upon this place, and upon the inhabitants thereof, even all the words of the book which the king of Judah hath read" (verses 15,16). Huldah goes on to say: "As touching the words which thou hast heard ..." (verse 18). What force the written Word can have on the lives of those who have ears to hear!

Tremble before the Word

The attitude of mind which Josiah had towards the Word is exactly that which the Lord delights in. Through Isaiah He said, "To this man will I look, even to him that is poor and of a contrite spirit, and trembleth at my word" (Isaiah 66:2). The Lord through Huldah said:

"Because thine heart was tender, and thou hast humbled thyself before the LORD, when thou heardest what I spake against this place, and against the inhabitants thereof, that they should become a desolation and a curse, and hast rent thy clothes, and wept before me; I also have heard thee, saith the LORD. Behold therefore, I will gather thee unto thy fathers, and thou shalt be gathered into thy grave in peace; and thine eyes shall not see all the evil which I will bring upon this place." (verses 19,20)

Josiah's attitude towards the Scriptures is one which we all must cultivate. In our children we need to develop a respect for the Word at the youngest age. We should teach them to handle the Bible carefully, though it should not become an object of superstitious reverence. It is a precious thing which in many parts of the world is in very short supply. When we sit down to do the readings we need an atmosphere of calm and seriousness, not casualness or flippancy. We need to read prayerfully, conscious that we are reading the words of the Creator of heaven and earth.

The same attitude of mind will ensure that we are first hearers before we are speakers. We shall listen to what the Scriptures say, "rightly dividing the word of truth". An essential part of that is to look for accurate translation. Ease of understanding of an English translation is a poor criterion for choosing a version if what we are finding easy to understand is not what God intended. Is it not the case that only when we have studied a passage carefully, comparing Scripture with Scripture and using the concordance and lexicon, do we have a good idea which translation gives the best sense? We should also bear in mind that there are things revealed in the Word which are not easy to understand. We may feel that if only we could get hold of the right version all would be plain. But Peter says of Paul's epistles that there are in them "some things hard to be understood", and then he goes on to say, "which they that are unlearned and unstable wrest, as they do also the other scriptures, unto their own destruction" (2 Peter 3:16).

The essential thing is to find out to the best of our ability what the Creator has revealed, and humble ourselves before it. When we find, as so often we will, that the Word is not in line with the trends in society, such as in the case of the role of women in the ecclesia, or the sanctity of marriage, or the warning against the "love of money", then we must align ourselves with the Word and not try to find translations or paraphrases or commentators which wrongly dilute the force of the Word or undermine the authority of the prophets and apostles who wrote it under inspiration of the Spirit of God.

Every Word Matters

The expression used by Josiah and then by Huldah, "the words of this book", draws attention to the verbal inspiration of Scripture. It is not just that all Scripture is given by God in the sense that the general message is right, but that every word of the original revelation is God's chosen expression and consequently the resulting Scripture is "spirit and life". This understanding of the nature of inspiration is a vital truth upon which not only our doctrines are built but also from which follows our approach to Bible study. We can follow themes through

Scripture which span hundreds of years in their compilation just because all Scripture is given by God. We can do word studies and search for the most accurate rendering of a passage just because every word is intended to be there for a purpose, revealing the mind of God.

An example of this very point is to be found in the passage under consideration. When we look at Huldah's reply to Josiah we notice that her mode of address is hardly deferential: "Tell the man that sent you unto me ..." (2 Kings 22:15). Why did she call Josiah "the man" and not "the king" as she does later (verse 18)? The answer may be found in the book of Deuteronomy which had just been rediscovered. There, in chapter 17, is the passage which describes how Israel were to appoint their king. It would have been a passage Josiah would have read many times, perhaps stopping Shaphan at that point on the first occasion he heard it and getting him to reread it. We can say with some certainty that Josiah paid particular attention to this chapter because the records in 2 Kings 22 and 2 Chronicles 34 both quote from it.

Notice the sequence of thought in Deuteronomy 17. First comes the account of what to do in matters of judgement. The difficult cases were to be brought to the priests and Levites and to the judge (e.g. Samuel). The verdict was binding and the people had to do what they were told: "Thou shalt not decline from the sentence which they shall shew thee, to the right hand, nor to the left" (verse 11). Then comes the warning: "And the man that will do presumptuously, and will not hearken ... even that man shall die" (verse 12). Immediately after this is the record about choosing a king: "When thou art come into the land ... and shalt say, I will set a king over me ..." The king was to be one of their own nation and he was not to multiply horses or wives or gold. On the positive side there was something very significant that he should do: "And it shall be, when he sitteth upon the throne of his kingdom, that he shall write him a copy of this law in a book out of that which is before the priests the Levites: and it shall be with him, and he shall read therein all the days of his life: that he may learn to fear the LORD his God, to keep all the words of this law and these statutes, to do them" (verses

18,19). The reason given for this instruction was "that his heart be not lifted up above his brethren" (verse 20).

Make the Bible your own

As Josiah heard these words he would immediately know what he had to do, which was to make his very own copy of the Law. Did he do it? In the context of Deuteronomy 17 we can rephrase the question: Would he be presumptuous and refuse? Huldah's reply to Josiah can now be seen to have a special force: "Tell *the man* ..." Here is a warning from Deuteronomy 17:12: *"The man* that will do presumptuously ..." For however regal the court of the throne of David had become over the years, the king was someone who had been taken from his brethren, "a man" of the same human nature as all others, and he needed to be reminded of this by a daily reading of the Word, "that his heart be not lifted up above his brethren". Huldah's words are reinforced by further references to Deuteronomy. Evil was going to come on Judah "because they have forsaken" the Lord (see Deuteronomy 28:20). "The LORD shall send upon thee cursing ... because of the wickedness of thy doings, whereby thou hast forsaken me." The people had "burned incense to other gods" (see Deuteronomy 31:18,20) and therefore they would become "a desolation and a curse" (see Deuteronomy 28:15,45).

Did Josiah make his personal copy of the Law as commanded? The answer to the question can be inferred from the text. Deuteronomy 17 goes on to say that the daily reading of the Word would have the result that the king would "turn not aside from the commandment, to the right hand, or to the left" (verse 20). It is these words which are quoted in the historical records. The account in 2 Kings 22 begins: "And he did that which was right in the sight of the LORD, and walked in all the way of David his father, and turned not aside to the right hand or to the left" (verse 2). The same is to be found in 2 Chronicles 34:2. The inspired record is leading us to see in Josiah a king whose life is summarised by Deuteronomy 17:20. Indeed there was no king before or since amongst the kings of Judah who did "according to all the law of Moses" (2 Kings 23:25). The picture we have, then, of Josiah is of a man who made his own personal and treasured copy of Scripture from which he read "all the days of his life".

We have already mentioned the fact that the great discovery of the Law was shared with others, most notably the prophet Jeremiah. It would seem likely that royal Bible classes were set up to read and expound the Word. Looking back to this time, Jeremiah recalls: "Thy words were found, and I did eat them; and thy word was unto me the joy and rejoicing of mine heart: for I am called by thy name, O LORD God of hosts" (Jeremiah 15:16). To understand what Jeremiah meant about his relation to God's name we need to go to the beginning of his prophecy. When Jeremiah was called to prophesy he pleaded that he was too young, but the answer came back: "Say not, I am a child ... whatsoever I command thee thou shalt speak ... I have put my words in thy mouth" (Jeremiah 1:7-9). These words come from Deuteronomy 18:18 where the Lord says to Moses: "I will raise them up a Prophet from among their brethren, like unto thee, and will put my words in his mouth; and he shall speak unto them all that I shall command him." As Jeremiah read from this book he would surely have taken a particular interest in this passage. He was called to prophesy five years before the book was discovered, but when he was able to read it he would see chapter 18 was his chapter, just as chapter 17 was Josiah's. He was not that special "prophet" referred to but he certainly came in the same Spirit; and the Lord had quoted those very words of Deuteronomy 18:18 of him. Jeremiah was a prophet of the sort described in verse 19, of whom the Lord had said, "he shall speak in my name". It was this association with the God whose name means "I will be" that so thrilled Jeremiah.

Gems of Bible Study

Just as Josiah made the discovery of the Law by Hilkiah in the treasury of the house of God his own personal and treasured discovery, so should we. And if we, like Jeremiah, have a consuming interest in its message it will become the joy and rejoicing of our hearts also.

The Lord Jesus Christ teaches us to consider the Gospel message contained in the Scriptures as a great treasure to be discovered: "Again the kingdom of heaven is like unto treasure hid in a field; the which when a man hath found, he hideth, and for joy thereof goeth and selleth all that he hath, and buyeth that field. Again the kingdom of heaven is like unto a merchant man, seeking goodly pearls: who, when he had found one pearl of great price, went and sold all that he had, and bought it" (Matthew 13:44-46). The force of this parable applies to each of us. Where treasure of silver and gold is concerned, it can be discovered and hidden by only one or two and the rest are no better off. But the treasure of the Gospel can be discovered by everyone and its worth is still undiminished. Each of us who has come to the Truth has discovered a treasure, and that is the way we should look at it. It is a matter of personal appreciation of the Word of God. It does not matter how many times the same thoughts have been discovered before by others, they remain precious pearls of great price. It does not matter if we have learned them by direct personal study or by instruction from another. Once those thoughts are appreciated they become our thoughts: God's Word treasured in our hearts, and no man can rob us of that.

The Master goes on to recount another parable introduced by the words, "Have ye understood all these things? They say unto him, Yea, Lord" (Matthew 13:51). If they truly have understood, what should follow? The Lord answers this with the parable: "Then said he unto them, Therefore every scribe which is instructed unto the kingdom of heaven is like unto a man that is an householder, which bringeth forth out of his treasure things new and old" (verse 52). Was the Lord thinking here of Shaphan who did not at first seem to appreciate the significance of the discovery of the book? Were the disciples in a comparable state of ignorance? They had professed that they understood and the Lord showed them the responsibility of that profession.

The householder who shows his guests his precious treasures is the Bible student (the scribe) sharing the wonders of the Word which he has discovered: "things new and old". He will have discovered things already known by others – "old" things – but that does not take anything away from their beauty. Far from it, their value increases with age. If someone else has already discovered the point, we should not be disappointed. It is now more likely to be correct! "New" discoveries may well turn out to be wrong exposition. How many of us have seen a 'tremendous' point in a passage only to find that on further investigation we have looked up the wrong word in the lexicon! Novelty is not what makes our discoveries valuable. However well known a thing is, in the end, just like the Gospel message itself, it has to be appreciated personally.

We make a big mistake if we are setting out to be different, trying to say something new – like the Athenians of old, who "spent their time in nothing else, but either to tell, or to hear some new thing" (Acts 17:21). Paul refers to those who "will not endure sound doctrine" as having "itching ears" (2 Timothy 4:3), wanting to have their ears tickled. The "new" things which the scripturally educated scribe expounds are not the sort of ear tickling novelties which in the end are either chaff which blows away or cancerous growths on the body which destroy spiritual health (see 2 Timothy 2:17). New things can indeed be discovered, but these arise out of "old" things. Their veracity is tested by their relation to the certainties of the covenants and promises already known. In presenting our studies, we should build up the thoughts as Scripture directs, not falling into the trap of omitting the well known because it is well known – by some. We need to remember that our young people and the visitor, or the newly baptized who have not come from Christadelphian families, will not have heard before what we may be taking for granted.

If the householder of the parable is the faithful Bible student or scribe, and the precious jewels are the gems of the Word discovered by Bible study, where is the treasury out of which the householder produces them? In Matthew 12 the Lord has already given us the answer: "A good man out of *the good treasure of the heart* bringeth forth good things: and an evil man out of the evil treasure bringeth forth evil things" (verse 35). Bible study is a matter of the heart, as it most certainly was for Josiah and Jeremiah. Only when the teacher has himself been convinced and moved by the things he has found, can he speak with conviction. And it is this conviction which plays a big part in being able to demonstrate the beauty of "things new and old". A speaker who has plagiarised another will have to be a good actor to be convincing; but even if the thoughts we are offering have been learned from others, so long as they are scriptural and they have become our own thoughts then their beauty is undiminished.

9

A NEW COVENANT

"And the king sent, and they gathered unto him all the elders of Judah and of Jerusalem. And the king went up into the house of the LORD, and all the men of Judah and all the inhabitants of Jerusalem with him, and the priests, and the prophets, and all the people, both small and great: and he read in their ears all the words of the book of the covenant which was found in the house of the LORD."   (2 Kings 23:1,2)

THIS was the reaction of Josiah to the message from Huldah whom he had consulted about the discovery of the book of the Law. The book is referred to significantly as the "book of the covenant". The section of Deuteronomy which so engaged Josiah's attention, the curses of Deuteronomy chapters 27 and 28, were summed up by Moses in this way: "These are the words of the covenant, which the LORD commanded Moses to make with the children of Israel in the land of Moab, beside the covenant which he made with them in Horeb" (Deuteronomy 29:1). The phrase "the book of the covenant" is drawing attention very clearly to this section of Scripture.

But what exactly was this covenant described in Deuteronomy? As with the covenant made with Israel at Sinai it was also a covenant based upon commandments which had to be kept. It had to do with the instruction to the people that when they entered into the land and came to Mount Ebal they were to build an altar and write upon the stones "all the words of this law very plainly" (Deuteronomy 27:8). A selection of those statutes were then to be proclaimed in the form of "curses" and the people were to reply to each statement with an "Amen". The selection of commandments is very interesting, beginning with the worship of God and moving on first to respect for parents and then to love for one's neighbour. These curses covered idolatry, despising parents, cheating a person of his inheritance by removing landmarks, making the "blind to wander out of the way", and perverting the judgement of the stranger, fatherless and widow. After these followed four curses to do with sexual immorality and then came curses to do with secretly smiting a neighbour and taking bribes to pervert the course of justice. The last of the twelve was: "Cursed be he that confirmeth not all the words of this law to do them. And all the people shall say, Amen" (verse 26).

This last curse has a very important significance which is explained by the Apostle Paul in Galatians: "For as many as are of the works of the law are under the curse: for it is written, Cursed is every one that continueth not in all things which are written in the book of the law to do them" (3:10). In pronouncing this curse Israel had inevitably consigned themselves to falling foul of it, because it implied perfect obedience to the works of law. Even 99.9% success was not acceptable under this edict. As James explains: "For whosoever shall keep the whole law, and yet offend in one point, he is guilty of all" (2:10). Here was a precept deliberately designed to demonstrate to Israel that salvation by the successful adherence to law was impossible.

A Different Covenant

The covenant of Deuteronomy 27–29, though similar to that given at Sinai in certain respects, was said however to be a different covenant. In which way did it differ? First of all of course the people entering into this covenant were only children at Sinai if they were there at all. The later covenant in Moab was their very own covenant by which they were shown to be God's special people: "Take heed, and hearken, O Israel; this day thou art become the people of the LORD thy God" (27:9). But there was another and new addition to this covenant which separated it from the covenant at Sinai. Israel were not left to consider merely the negative aspects resulting from the failure to obtain perfect obedience. They were at the same time to be reminded of the means by which they could be saved, by the faith of Abraham.

It is an important point to bear in mind when we consider Israel under the Law that they also had the opportunity for faith. It is often asked whether people in Israel actually understood the Gospel in Old Testament times and how many will be in the Kingdom. The question is understandable because the Law could only promise blessings of mortal existence in the land during their lifetime. It could not bring eternal life. But we should not overlook a basic truth that all the while the Law was in force so were the promises to Abraham. Paul says as much in Galatians: "And this I say, that the covenant, that was confirmed before of God in Christ, the law, which was four hundred and thirty years after, cannot disannul, that it should make the promise of none effect" (3:17).

How many in Israel understood these principles we cannot say, but Moses certainly draws their attention to them in Moab. He says: "That thou shouldest enter into covenant with the LORD thy God ... that he may establish thee today for a people unto himself, and that he may be unto thee a God, as he hath said unto thee, and as he hath sworn unto thy fathers, to Abraham, to Isaac, and to Jacob" (Deuteronomy 29:12,13). The words of Moses pick out a reference to Genesis 17:7: "And I will establish my covenant between me and thee and thy seed after thee in their generations for an everlasting covenant, to be a God unto thee, and to thy seed after thee." In so doing Moses sets the covenant in Moab in the context of the everlasting covenant to Abraham. It must be acknowledged that the Lord never intended that Israel should keep the Law as a means of achieving salvation through works. The Lord would certainly know from the outset that that was impossible. The only other way to keep the Law was through faith. Not that perfect obedience would have been possible even for Abraham, but faith would enable Israelites to see the spirit of the Law which they would follow from a heartfelt desire to honour the One who had made such wonderful promises to them. In this way, as for the disciple of Christ, keeping the commandments would be an expression of faith.

74

A Covenant based on Love

It would appear then that what we have recorded in Deuteronomy 27 onwards is a progression of thought similar to that developed by Paul in Romans. The first point made is that all are under sin because of failure to attain to perfect obedience. Israel would learn this as they suffered the consequences of disobedience which are set out in Deuteronomy 29:21-29. But the question must then be answered, how can sinners be saved? The answer is through the faith which was manifest by Abraham in the God who made great and precious promises. In Deuteronomy 30, Moses shows how this would happen for Israel. In captivity they would call to mind the covenant which they had broken and would turn to the Lord "with all thine heart, and with all thy soul" (verse 2). Then He would have compassion on them: "And the LORD thy God will circumcise thine heart, and the heart of thy seed, to love the LORD thy God with all thine heart, and with all thy soul" (verse 6). Israel would then be brought back to the land once again, under covenant relationship through which they would receive the blessings and not the curses promised (verse 9) if they "keep his commandments and his statutes which are written in this book of the law, and if thou turn unto the LORD thy God with all thine heart, and with all thy soul" (verse 10).

The progression in this section of Deuteronomy from works of law to works of faith is confirmed by the apostle's interpretation of this Scripture. We have already seen that Paul teaches that Deuteronomy 27:26 is a proof that "no man is justified by the law in the sight of God" (Galatians 3:11). But in writing to the Romans Paul also comments on Deuteronomy 30:11-14. He introduces the quotation with the words: "But the righteousness which is of faith speaketh on this wise ..." (Romans 10:6). The commandment (or "word") which Moses says was near unto them was in fact a prophecy of the Lord Jesus Christ!

These are some of the things which Josiah must have been pondering as he called the people together.

A Broken Covenant

When Josiah read the book of Deuteronomy he realised that the nation had broken the covenant and therefore were bringing the curses recorded there upon themselves. It wasn't just that they failed to keep the Law perfectly, but that they had despised the Law and turned away from Yahweh to serve other gods. The coming judgement was certain, and though it would not happen in his lifetime it could not be averted. Josiah must have understood and accepted this. So what was he attempting to do by making a new covenant? Was he witnessing against that nation? Was he seeking to influence the remnant that would respond?

The key to our understanding of these events is Jeremiah's prophecy. It has been shown in other studies* how closely Jeremiah's words are linked to the section of Deuteronomy we are considering. In relation to the covenant Jeremiah says: "Hear ye the words of this covenant, and speak unto the men of Judah, and to the inhabitants of Jerusalem; and say unto them, Thus saith the LORD God of Israel; Cursed be the man that obeyeth not the words of this covenant, which I commanded your fathers in the day that I brought them forth out of the land of Egypt, from the iron furnace, saying, Obey my voice, and do them, according to all which I command you: so shall ye be my people, and I will be your God" (Jeremiah 11:2-4). This reference is so close to Deuteronomy 27:26, it seems it was the covenant in Moab to which the prophet was referring. This conclusion is given weight by the reply of Jeremiah: "Then answered I, and said, So be it (i.e. Amen), O LORD" (verse 5). Here Jeremiah echoes the response which Israel were to give at Mount Ebal.

Jeremiah was commanded to preach these words in the streets of Jerusalem, saying, "Hear ye the words of this covenant, and do them" (verse 6). It would seem likely that the passage in Jeremiah 11 was contemporary with Josiah's reformation of 2 Kings 23 (although it is curious that Jeremiah does not appear to make any direct reference to it in the prophecy). The prophet was reinforcing the very thing which Josiah was trying to achieve. But Jeremiah goes on to make a very interesting though sad comment upon the response of the people to

*Brother T. J. Barling, "The Ministry of Jeremiah", *The Christadelphian*, 1994, page 101).

this reformation. He says: "And the LORD said unto me, A conspiracy is found among the men of Judah, and among the inhabitants of Jerusalem. They are turned back to the iniquities of their forefathers, which refused to hear my words; and they went after other gods to serve them: the house of Israel and the house of Judah have broken my covenant which I made with their fathers" (verses 9,10).

The reference to a conspiracy is revealing. Why did they need to conspire? So many times in Israel's history the idolatry of the people was blatant and overt. "A conspiracy" lends weight to the dating of the prophecy to the time of Josiah's covenant. The people were duplicitous. Outwardly they were conforming to the policy of their Godly king. Privately they were just the same as before. The most telling of all the statements in Jeremiah is that in 3:10: "And yet for all this her treacherous sister Judah hath not turned unto me with her whole heart, but feignedly, saith the LORD."

It is indeed sad to realise that when the people gathered before the temple, what appeared to be a wholehearted and sincere conversion was for most an expediency to humour the king. "And the king stood by a pillar, and made a covenant before the LORD, to walk after the LORD, and to keep his commandments and his testimonies and his statutes with all their heart and all their soul, to perform the words of this covenant that were written in this book. And all the people stood to the covenant" (2 Kings 23:3). Note that the word "their" is in italics in the phrase "with all *their* heart and with all *their* soul"; it does not appear in the original text. The hearts and souls of the people were not in the covenant. They should have been. This was the spirit of Deuteronomy 30 (see verses 6 and 10). But the newly discovered Word had not entered into good and honest hearts. The parallel record in 2 Chronicles 34:31 is striking. It is almost exactly the same, word for word, with the exception that instead of "with all their heart, and with all their soul" it has: "And the king stood in his place, and made a covenant before the LORD ... to keep his commandments, and his testimonies, and his statutes, with all his heart, and with all his soul." Whatever deception the people were perpetrating there was not a shadow of doubt about the sincerity of their king.

The New Covenant

Despite the failure of Josiah and Jeremiah to convert the nation, the efforts to re-establish the covenant with Israel provided a fitting backcloth for the wonderful promise of the new covenant which the Lord Jesus Christ would confirm in his own blood. In chapter 31 of the prophecy the Lord says:

> "Behold, the days come, saith the LORD, that I will make a new covenant with the house of Israel, and with the house of Judah: not according to the covenant that I made with their fathers in the day that I took them by the hand to bring them out of the land of Egypt; which my covenant they brake, although I was an husband unto them, saith the LORD: but this shall be the covenant that I will make with the house of Israel; after those days, saith the LORD, I will put my law in their inward parts, and write it in their hearts; and will be their God, and they shall be my people. And they shall teach no more every man his neighbour, and every man his brother, saying, Know the LORD: for they shall all know me, from the least of them unto the greatest of them, saith the LORD: for I will forgive their iniquity, and I will remember their sin no more."
>
> (Jeremiah 31:31-34)

What a striking contrast with the hypocritical lip service which the nation was paying to the covenant of Josiah. From the beginning of their tenancy of the land God wanted His people to serve Him out of love. "See, I have set before thee this day life and good, and death and evil; in that I command thee this day to love the LORD thy God ..." (Deuteronomy 30:15,16). To serve from love would be to respond to the mercy they had been shown with heart and soul, just as Josiah had done. But Israel, even when they were not overtly following idols, missed the point of their calling. Only a few could appreciate that "to love him with all the heart, and with all the understanding, and with all the soul, and with all the strength, and to love his neighbour as himself, is more than all whole burnt offerings and sacrifices" (Mark 12:33).

As Deuteronomy 30 indicated, it would only be after the chastening experiences of captivity, persecution and wandering amongst the nations that the Jews would return to their God. Only then would God circumcise their heart "to love the LORD thy God with all thine heart, and with all thy soul" (verse 6). The process of conversion of natural Israel is described in detail in other places where the prophet describes how God will give Israel a new heart and a new spirit (Ezekiel 36:26). When the Lord Jesus returns with the saints to deliver Jerusalem from annihilation (Zechariah 14) those that survive will accept the Lord as their Messiah and Saviour (Zechariah 12:10). No longer will they observe statutes and ordinances in outward ritual from motives of pride, but the spirit of the Law will be impressed upon their hearts and minds.

Furthermore: "They shall teach no more every man his neighbour, and every man his brother, saying, Know the LORD: for they shall all know me, from the least of them unto the greatest of them." In Jeremiah's time we are told that "from the least of them even unto the greatest of them every one is given to covetousness" (Jeremiah 6:13); but no longer. Josiah had anticipated this all-embracing scope of the Gospel of the New Covenant when he called "all" the people together. 2 Kings 23:2 says, "both small and great" – or as the margin gives it, "from small even unto great". The parallel record in 2 Chronicles 34:30 puts it around the other way, "from great even unto small". Put side by side these passages have a beautiful symmetry which emphasises the universal appeal of the Gospel.

Set against the times of Josiah, the new covenant promised in Jeremiah 31 can be seen to apply specifically to the natural seed of Abraham, Isaac and Jacob, who will be converted to become spritually-minded when the Lord Jesus Christ returns to reign over them. The opening of the covenant to the Gentiles, for which we are so thankful, is only possible because through faith and baptism into the Lord Jesus Christ, Gentiles become adopted into the commonwealth of Israel and the covenants of promise (Ephesians 2:12). This privilege which has preceded the conversion of the natural seed in no way diminishes the application of the prophecy to the Jews.

For us, however, the new covenant is something which we entered at our baptism. Christ has achieved for us what the Law could not do in that it was weak through the flesh. The new covenant in the blood of Christ brings upon us the blessing of Abraham, the forgiveness of sins (see Romans 4). But we who are so privileged should be sure to learn the lessons from the times of Josiah. "This cup is the new covenant in my blood", said the Lord; and Paul adds, "But let a man examine himself, and so let him eat of that bread, and drink of that cup". The covenant must be a matter of heart and soul and not mere outward observance or rhetoric. The Word of God which we treasure must not become an antique. It must be written upon our hearts and minds, "written not with ink, but with the Spirit of the living God; not in tables of stone, but in the fleshy tables of the heart" (2 Corinthians 3:3). It is the spirit of the Word, as opposed to the letter of the Law, that the apostle is referring to. It can be summarised in the words of the new covenant – "Know the LORD". What this means is to know the character of the Father through experiencing His love and then manifesting His attributes in our lives. Josiah was an excellent example of this. The Lord says of him, "He judged the cause of the poor and needy; then it was well with him: was not this to know me? saith the LORD" (Jeremiah 22:16).

10

VESSELS FIT FOR DESTRUCTION

THE proposition that there were two distinct cleansings of the land by Josiah (see Chapter 5) may not be readily accepted by all. The evidence is based on a close comparison of the two records in 2 Kings and 2 Chronicles. The first cleansing recorded in 2 Chronicles 34:3 says that "in the twelfth year" of his reign Josiah "began to purge Judah and Jerusalem". The record goes on to describe Josiah breaking up and pulverising the altars and other trappings of idol worship. Verse 6 then recounts how the purge was extended northward into the territory once occupied by the ten tribes. When this was done, "when he had broken down the altars and the groves, and had beaten the graven images into powder, and cut down all the idols throughout all the land of Israel, he returned to Jerusalem". The account is of a single though prolonged campaign beginning in the temple in Jerusalem and finishing in Galilee. Verse 7 shows that all the land was included in the campaign. Verse 8 indicates that the work had been done to Josiah's satisfaction and he returned to repair the house: "Now in the eighteenth year of his reign, when he had purged the land, and the house ..."

The second cleansing recorded in 2 Kings 23 is much more detailed than the Chronicles record and is positioned after the king had returned to Jerusalem and the book of the Law was discovered in the eighteenth year of Josiah's reign. It has been pointed out that some of the details described in 2 Kings 23 about the removal of the altars and so on would have caused structural damage to the temple and would therefore have been carried out before the repairs to the house mentioned in chapter 22 were undertaken. But, as mentioned previously, the suggestion that there was indeed a second cleansing after the discovery of the Law is confirmed by 2 Kings 23:24. This passage describes Josiah's motivation for his second campaign – that "he might perform the words of the law which were written in the book that Hilkiah the priest found in the house of the LORD".

It should also be noted that a straightforward reading of the text of 2 Kings 23 does not allow for a break in the flow of events beginning with the calling of the nation to the renewal of the covenant:

"The king sent, and they gathered unto him all the elders of Judah and Jerusalem ..." (verse 1)

"And the king went up into the house of the LORD ..." (verse 2)

"And the king stood by a pillar, and made a covenant ..." (verse 3)

"And the king commanded Hilkiah the high priest, and the priests of the second order, and the keepers of the door, to bring forth out of the temple of the LORD all the vessels that were made for Baal, and for the grove, and for all the host of heaven: and he burned them without Jerusalem in the fields of Kidron, and carried the ashes of them unto Bethel." (verse 4)

Vessels of Wood and Earth

Interestingly there is no mention in the 2 Chronicles record of the vessels of the temple. At that time Josiah dealt with the altars, groves and images. Now he was dealing with those things which might easily have been hidden from view when he began the cleansing. Removal of these vessels would not, one would imagine, involve structural damage to the newly repaired temple.

The vessels in question had been specially crafted for the worship of Baal (the Canaanite fertility god which had been introduced into the northern tribes by Jezebel) and for the grove (the Asherah) and for the host of heaven. The latter were among those things specifically warned against in the Law. Moses had said, "Take ye therefore good heed unto yourselves ... lest thou lift up thine eyes unto heaven, and when thou seest the sun, and the moon, and the stars, even all the host of heaven, shouldest be driven to worship them" (Deuteronomy 4:15,19). But that is exactly what Israel and Judah did.

This cult seems to have flourished in Judah particularly in the reign of Manasseh (2 Kings 21:3). An insight into what was involved can be gained from the Assyrian stone stelae, some of which are in the British Museum, depicting the kings of Assyria standing beneath the symbols of the host of heaven. In the illustration the king can be seen clicking his fingers (a mark of homage!) to salute the horned helmet of the supreme deity Ashur, the winged disc of the sun god Shamash, the moon god Sin, the lightning fork of the weather god Adad, and the star of Ishtar, the goddess of love and war.* Changes in the positions of the planets were interpreted in relation to the

will of the gods and used to predict forthcoming events. Involved in the worship of these deities was the burning of incense on the rooftops and the pouring out of drink offerings, as mentioned in Jeremiah 19:13. It would have been the vessels used for this sort of thing that were removed from the house of Yahweh.

Worship of Sun, Moon and Stars

Jeremiah referred to the hold which this cult had over the people. He foresaw the time when the bones of those who worshipped the stars and planets would be exhumed and mockingly spread before the very things which they had worshipped: "And they shall spread them before the sun, and the moon, and all the host of heaven whom they have loved, and whom they have served, and after whom they have walked, and whom they have sought, and whom they have worshipped" (8:2). How terrible is the intensity of

---

* Information from Julian Reade in *Assyrian Sculpture*, British Museum Publications, 1987.

their devotion. Note the verbs used – love, serve, walk, seek, worship. If only Israel could have applied such dedication and single-mindedness to the worship of Yahweh! If only people today would take as much daily interest in the Word of God and the signs of the times as many show in the horoscopes of the modern day stargazers.

In Scripture, vessels are symbols of people who should be dedicated to the service of God. It is a metaphor that the Apostle Paul develops: "In a great house there are not only vessels of gold and of silver, but also of wood and of earth; and some to honour, and some to dishonour. If a man therefore purge himself from these, he shall be a vessel unto honour, sanctified, and meet for the master's use, and prepared unto every good work" (2 Timothy 2:20,21). God is not content to use for His purposes any vessel: He requires those that have been sanctified and set apart from the polluting influences of the world.

Josiah certainly was a vessel unto honour, as he sought to turn the nation to true worship. The responsibility of removing the dishonourable vessels was given to the "high priest, and the priests of the second order, and the keepers of the door". The high priest was the one who was to lead the process. Who better to distinguish the true from the false? Our High Priest will do the same thing, as Paul says to Timothy, "The Lord knoweth them that are his". The other priests, "of the second order", may refer to those priests who lived in the "college" or second quarter of the city (2 Kings 22:14). The word "second" is interesting inasmuch as it is the same word rendered "copy" in Deuteronomy 17:18. (Were they the priests given the task of copying the Law? At any rate they would have reminded Josiah of his solemn duty to make the Bible his own, and they serve to remind us that the work of discerning the true vessels from the false in the house of God can only be conducted properly by a wise application of the Scriptures of truth.) The third group given the job of removing the vessels were the doorkeepers. Theirs was the responsibility to control who (which "vessels") were allowed into the house of God, a responsibility which still has to be carried out today through the careful interview of applicants for baptism and the application of scriptural principles to those who "walk disorderly" or who hold to false doctrines.

The pagan vessels were taken outside the city to the Kidron valley and there burned. For this to be possible the vessels must have been made "of wood or earth" – vessels of dishonour in 2 Timothy 2 – and the ashes carried to Bethel. The reason for going to Bethel must be to do with the fact that Bethel was made the centre of the apostasy by Jeroboam. It would represent a very strong message to the people that Josiah was intent on undoing the evil that Jeroboam the son of Nebat had introduced.

The next event recorded is the removal of the idolatrous priest (2 Kings 23:5). These were the "Chemarim" who had been ordained to burn incense in the high places to Baal and the sun, moon and stars. The word is used only three times in Scripture. In Hosea 10:5 it identifies the priests who ministered to the calf worship cult in the northern kingdom. In Zephaniah 1:4 it refers to the same people Josiah is dealing with. The word "chemarim" is derived from another which in Lamentations 5:10 is translated "black" and it has been suggested that the Chemarim got their name from wearing black robes.

"Sanctified" for Destruction

After dealing with the idolatrous priests, whose continued presence in Judah would have been a threat to true worship, Josiah "brought out the grove from the house of the LORD" (2 Kings 23:6) and burned it at Kidron. Not only that, but he "stamped it small to powder, and cast the powder thereof upon the graves of the children of the people". If this event was carried out after Josiah returned to Jerusalem, and is not a repetition of earlier events, then it shows the seriousness of the conspiracy which was working against Josiah's reforms.* The "grove" or "Asherah" was the central object of the fertility cult and it had been set up in the house of Yahweh: "the grove of trees, with a stripped and sculpted tree in the middle of it"

---

* In support of this view is the observation that in the earlier cleansings in 2 Chronicles 34:4 the groves etc. were broken down in the presence of the king, but in the 2 Kings 23 record it is Josiah himself who is said to have carried out the work.

was dedicated to the worship of Asherah, the mother-goddess. Asherah was also identified with Ishtar and Astarte the goddess of love. In all probability it was this female deity that Jeremiah refers to in 44:17 as "the queen of heaven".

In association with the Asherah the priests had set up "houses of the sodomites, that were by the house of the LORD, where the women wove hangings for the grove" (2 Kings 23:7). The sodomites, as the English rendering of the Hebrew *qadesh* implies, were male prostitutes employed by the people in the worship of Baal. The Hebrew word is derived from *qadash* which means holy or sanctified! The feminine equivalent of this is the word for a harlot. In the very house of the Holy One of Israel had been set up a cult which was "sanctified" or set apart for the things which are abomination in the sight of God. To adorn the booths where these despicable things were going on, the women had woven "hangings" and so were accomplices to this male perversity.

The setting up of the Asherah in the temple was the greatest insult to God it was possible to make, but it may have had a more subtle intention. Archaeological evidence* has been uncovered which shows that before the time of Josiah the worship of "Yahweh" had been paganised, though preserving the name itself. Inscriptions have been found in southern Palestine with such things as "I have blessed you by Yahweh of Samaria and his Asherah" and "I have blessed thee by Yahweh ... and his Asherah: may he bless thee and keep thee, and may he be with my lord". Here Asherah is presented as the wife of Yahweh. In this way the One True God had been reduced in the minds of the worshippers to the ranks of the pagan deities and replaced in His own house by a counterfeit. The justification for placing the Asherah in the temple would then be that it was Yahweh's Asherah which was to be worshipped. In this way the Chemarim would not only steal the name of the God of Israel but replace the true doctrines of the nature and character and purpose of God with the vile doctrines of men.

---

* Described in "The Asherah of 'Yahweh'", *The Testimony*, 1982, pages 173,174.

There are obvious parallels between the apostasy in Judah as described above, and modern day Christianity which purports to be based upon the Bible and to worship the God of the Bible, yet has substituted notions of deity borrowed from ancient Greek and other philosophies. Clearly, the use of the correct name in itself is no guarantee that the understanding is correct. The evangelical movement lays great stress on the idea of calling upon the name of "Jesus". But the one whom they imagine they are calling upon – the second person of the Trinity – does not correspond to the Son of God in heaven, and therefore they are not in reality calling upon Jesus at all.

After removing the Asherah, Josiah turned his attention to the land of Judah – from Geba to Beersheba. Again this differs from the first cleansing which concentrated on the northern territory – "the cities of Manasseh, and Ephraim, and Simeon, even unto Naphtali" – as the area of the work. Josiah this time removed the priests and destroyed the high places. These priests seem to have been Levitical priests who had misused their position as spiritual leaders. 2 Kings 23:9 says, "Nevertheless the priests of the high places came not up to the altar of the LORD in Jerusalem, but they did eat of the unleavened bread among their brethren". This was the situation the Law prescribed for any of the priestly family "that hath a blemish" (Leviticus 21:16-24) and it will be the position in the temple of the age to come as described by Ezekiel, for "the Levites that are gone away far from me, when Israel went astray ... after their idols ... they shall not come near unto me ... but they shall bear their shame" (44:10-13).

The priests who had defiled themselves by ministering to idols had a blemish which could not be removed and which necessarily affected what it was appropriate for them to do after the reformation. How could priests who had poured out incense to idols take on the prominent role before the nation of offering incense to Yahweh? An application of this principle can be seen in the apostolic injunction that bishops should be "blameless" (Titus 1:7), "moreover he must have a good report of them which are without; lest he fall into reproach and the snare of the devil" (1 Timothy 3:7).

The High Places of the Gates

The reference to "the high places of the gates that were in the entering in of the gate of Joshua the governor of the city" in 2 Kings 23:8 has been the source of some debate. One problem is that there is not known to have been a gate called the gate of Joshua in Jerusalem, although one writer has proposed that the place referred to was in fact in Beersheba. Another problem is that the phrase "high places of the gates" is in the plural, yet they appear to be located at one particular gate of the city, the gate of Joshua. The "high place" itself is generally considered to be an "elevated platform on which cultic objects were placed". Various explanations depending upon "correcting" the text have been proposed. Emerton* states that the most widely accepted theory is that a change in vowel pointing turns the "gates" into the "goats" or goat-demons, as in Leviticus 17:7. Emerton proposes that the "gates" referred to were an outer and inner gate at one entrance in the city wall, between which there was a shrine. He suggests that the "gate of Joshua" could refer to this entrance complex. The fact that "high place" is in the plural could perhaps indicate that there was an ecumenical centre for the worship of several deities at this gate.

Why are we given such details? Is it to contrast the idolatry which Josiah sought to remove with the work of a completely different sort of "Joshua" who will be the governor of New Jerusalem wherein dwelleth righteousness? And why are we given directions to identify the place – "which were on a man's left hand at the gate of the city"? The answer to this question can be found a little later where we are also given the location of the high places outside the city. Verse 13 refers to "the high places that were before Jerusalem, which were on the right hand of the mount of corruption". Here we have the possibilities for the ecumenical worshipper coming up to Jerusalem. On reaching the Mount of Olives he could turn

---

* Reviewed by J. A. Emerton in *The High Places of the Gates in 2 Kings XXIII 8, Vetus Testamentum XLIV*, 1994, pages 455–467.

right into the shrines built by Solomon for Ashtoreth, Chemosh and Milcom. If he didn't want to do that, once he got to the gate of the governor of the city he could turn left into the "high palaces of the gates", and afterwards he could go up to the temple to worship Yahweh.

This is the sort of thing Jeremiah said was going on in Jerusalem: "Will ye ... burn incense unto Baal, and walk after other gods whom ye know not; and come and stand before me in this house, which is called by my name, and say, We are delivered to do all these abominations?" (Jeremiah 7:9,10). Josiah was putting an end to such freedom of worship because it was deviating from the straight paths to the Kingdom of God. His own spiritual life is set in contrast to that of the nation: "He did that which was right in the sight of the LORD, and walked in all the way of David his father, and turned not aside to the right hand or to the left" (2 Kings 22:2).

The lesson from all this for ecclesial life today is surely obvious. Despite the ecumenical spirit of society and the "equal" treatment given to different "faiths" in religious education in schools, the disciple of Christ has only one place where he or she can go to worship and that is "the house of God, which is the ecclesia of the living God, the pillar and ground of the truth" (1 Timothy 3:15). It is no use arguing that since we now worship "in spirit and in truth" we can go to churches which may be attractive for various reasons, and still maintain our integrity. Would Josiah have attended one of the high places where incense was offered to another god?

11

THE CLEANSING CONTINUES

OUTSIDE Jerusalem on its southern side was a valley, called the valley of the son of Hinnom, which was particularly associated with the abominable practice of offering children as burnt offerings to the Ammonite god Molech. This practice was known from the earliest times of the nation of Israel. The Law had forbidden it (Leviticus 18:21), and anyone who indulged in it was to be put to death (20:2). The practice defiled God's sanctuary and profaned His holy name (verse 3).

The Blood of Innocents

Leviticus warns about turning a blind eye to it: "If the people of the land do any ways hide their eyes from the man, when he giveth of his seed unto Molech, and kill him not: then I will set my face against that man, and against his family, and will cut him off, and all that go a whoring after him, to commit whoredom with Molech, from among their people" (verses 4,5). The association between the worship of Molech and "whoredom", which was all too literal in the worship of these pagan deities, has suggested to some that the sacrifice of children may have been a way of disposing of unwanted pregnancies resulting from the whoredom. Infanticide was a well recognised form of population control in ancient times, much as abortion is today.

The worship of Molech with its child sacrifices was introduced into the nation by Solomon of all people (see 1 Kings 11:7), perhaps setting up the first high place in the valley of Hinnom. He was followed by Ahaz and by Manasseh. Interestingly, Jeremiah refers to the practice in association with the high place of Baal in the valley of Hinnom (Jeremiah 32:35). It seems that by the time of Josiah's reign there had been an ecumenical sharing of religious practices.

The location in the valley where these things were carried out was Tophet, thought to be at the junction of the valley of Hinnom and the Kidron valley. In chapter 7 of Jeremiah's prophecy, during the time of Josiah, the Lord deplores the fact that "they have built the high places of Tophet ... to burn their sons and their daughters in the fire; which I commanded them not, neither came it into my heart" (verse 31).* Jeremiah goes on to declare: "Therefore, behold, the days come, saith the LORD, that it shall no more be called Tophet, nor the valley of the son of Hinnom, but the valley of slaughter: for they shall bury in Tophet, till there be no place. And the carcases of this people shall be meat for the fowls of the heaven, and for the beasts of the earth" (verses 32,33).

Josiah clearly took very seriously the warnings of Jeremiah and Leviticus because "he defiled Topheth, which is in the valley of the children of Hinnom, that no man might make his son or his daughter to pass through the fire to Molech" (2 Kings 23:10). But no sooner had Josiah passed off the scene than Judah was once again practising the evil rite. In Jeremiah 19 the prophet is commanded to go to Tophet to pronounce judgement from the Lord: "Behold, I will bring evil upon this place, the which whosoever heareth, his ears shall tingle" (verse 3). The sacrifice of the children is referred to in the telling phrase "the blood of innocents", which emphasises the heinousness of the crime. Jeremiah has to break an earthen bottle in the valley to demonstrate what would happen to Jerusalem: "And they shall bury them in Tophet, till there be no place to bury" (verse 11).

Jeremiah describes the judgement on idolatrous Jerusalem with the words: "It shall burn, and shall not be quenched" (7:20). By New Testament times in fulfilment of this prophecy it seems that Tophet had long become a

---

* This last expression is repeated in a similar context in chapter 32:35. Were the people who did such things arguing that if God had asked Abraham to offer up Isaac then surely a human sacrifice was more pleasing than an animal one? But the offering of Isaac foreshadowed the willing sacrifice of the Lord Jesus, not offered to appease the wrath of deity but to declare the righteousness and love of God.

JOSIAH AND HIS CHILDREN

place where the refuse of the city was piled and the corpses of criminals were discarded.

The prophecy of Jeremiah provides an important background which highlights the significance of the words of the Lord Jesus when he was in Jerusalem and surrounded by the idolatry of a covetous nation. In the spirit of Josiah he had swept the temple clean, casting out the "idolaters" and even following the type of Josiah who commanded the vessels of idolatry to be taken out of the house of God. The Lord, says Mark, "would not suffer that any man should carry any vessel through the temple" (11:16), and he likened the place which was to be a house of prayer for all nations to the "den of thieves" described in Jeremiah 7. Matthew takes the parallels further as he goes on to recount the teaching of the Master at this time when he warned of the hypocrisy of the scribes and Pharisees. Hypocrisy was the character of worship in Josiah's time, as we have seen in Jeremiah 7: "Will ye steal, murder, and commit adultery, and swear falsely, and burn incense unto Baal, and walk after other gods whom ye know not; *and* come and stand before me in this house?" (verses 9,10).

One of the piercing observations in Matthew 23 seems to be a reference back to the inglorious history of Tophet, where the ever-burning rubbish heap which had such powerful historical associations was used by the Lord Jesus as a picture of eternal punishment, the Gehenna fire: "Woe unto you, scribes and Pharisees, hypocrites! for ye compass sea and land to make one proselyte, and when he is made, ye make him twofold more the child of hell (Gehenna) than yourselves" (verse 15). The children of the valley of Hinnom were those that were offered in sacrifice to Molech! The willing proselytes whom the Pharisees bound with zeal to the impossible burden of their tradition were doomed, and those who sacrificed them would suffer the judgements of which Jeremiah spoke, the unquenchable fire of Jerusalem's destruction, at the hand of the Romans – "ye serpents, ye generation of vipers, how can ye escape the damnation of hell (Gehenna)" (verse 33).

The Chariots of the Sun

After destroying Tophet, Josiah turned his attention to another feature of the idolatry of the city: "He took away the horses that the kings of Judah had given to the sun, at the entering in of the house of the LORD, by the chamber of Nathan-melech the chamberlain, which was in the suburbs, and burned the chariots of the sun with fire" (2 Kings 23:11). It has been suggested that these horses were real creatures stabled near the temple and used to pull special chariots in procession around the city in honour of the sun god. The location of the horses is given in detail – "by the chamber of Nathan-melech the chamberlain". The reason why we are given this detail is not immediately obvious since we do not read of this man anywhere else in the Scriptures. Is the reason to be found in the meaning of his name? "Nathan" is the Hebrew for 'to give' and "melech" is the word for 'king'. The name of the man emphasises the terrible truth that it was the kings of Judah who had devoted these creatures to the worship of the sun.

Nathan-melech was a eunuch (chamberlain) who had a room "at the entering in of the house of the LORD". We are then told that it was "in the suburbs". The word for "suburbs" is *parwarim* and this has been taken by lexicographers to be of foreign derivation. Gesenius suggests a Persian origin with the meaning of 'summer-house'. Another suggestion is that it derived from an Egyptian word for a portable chapel containing a divine image which was carried in festival processions. A more recent suggestion* has arisen out of the use of the word *parwar* in the Qumran Temple Scroll, which refers to a "columned area to the west side of the temple building where the sacrifices of the priests and the Israelites were kept separate". If this suggestion is true, then unclean animals dedicated to the worship of a pagan deity had been placed where clean sacrificial animals for the worship of the One true God should have been. These animals Josiah took away and then he burned the chariots

---

* Donna Runnalls, "The PARWAR: A Place of Ritual Separation?" *Vetus Testamentum*, XLI. 3 (1991), pages 324-331.

of the sun "with fire". What an appropriate way to signal the futility of the worship of that star.

The Altars of the Kings of Judah

Next in the list of Josiah's deeds is the reference to "the altars that were on the top of the upper chamber of Ahaz, which the kings of Judah had made, and the altars which Manasseh had made in the two courts of the house of the LORD" (2 Kings 23:12). The question which arises here is how these altars survived previous cleansings. The altars which Manasseh had made he himself tried to dispose of after his conversion: "He took away the strange gods, and the idol out of the house of the LORD, and all the altars that he had built in the mount of the house of the LORD, and in Jerusalem, and cast them out of the city" (2 Chronicles 33:15). It must have been the case, as we have pointed out previously, that someone had recovered the altars and hidden them for use when the storm had passed. The same thing could have happened during the first cleansing of Jerusalem by Josiah. Is the verse indicating that these altars were on the roof of a special chapel built by Ahaz, perhaps out of sight for secret worship, found now by Josiah because his zeal was intensified by the discovery of the Law? Zephaniah had warned that such secret worshippers would be found out: "I will cut off the remnant of Baal ... that worship the host of heaven upon the housetops" (1:4,5).

The Mount of Corruption

Outside Jerusalem on the Mount of Olives, known by Josiah as the Mount of Corruption, were the high places which Solomon built to "Ashtoreth the abomination of the Zidonians, and for Chemosh the abomination of the Moabites, and for Milcom the abomination of the children of Ammon" (2 Kings 23:13). The repeated use of the word "abomination" emphasises the filthy and despicable nature of idolatry in the sight of God. Solomon had built these places to please his foreign wives who had turned his heart away from serving Yahweh, the God of his father. How dangerous it is to marry out of the Truth! The high places Solomon built had a curious history. In the reign of Manasseh the Scripture records that "he built up again the high places which Hezekiah his father had destroyed;

and he reared up altars for Baal, and made a grove" (2 Kings 21:3). Did these "high places" include the ones originally built by Solomon? One cannot imagine that Hezekiah would have been content to view day by day across the Kidron valley the eyesores of idolatry which so shamed the memory of Solomon. But if he had pulled them down, the job had not been done properly. Manasseh it seems had been able to restore them. There is no record that after his conversion Manasseh tried to dismantle them. Perhaps the reformed king no longer had sufficient political power to remove them. That was left to Josiah.

Associated with the high places on the Mount of Olives which Josiah destroyed, there is a reference to the "images" and "groves" which Josiah broke down and "filled their places with the bones of men" (2 Kings 23:14). The Hebrew word translated "images" is *matstsebah* which Strong explains as 'something stationed, i.e. a column or (memorial stone)'. The high places, which were in effect pagan churches, had it seems both an asherah-pole and a matstsebah-pillar where also the bodies of priests and prophets were buried in honour. The poles were associated with the female sex symbol Asherah, and the pillars with the male deity Baal, the two figures together representing the husband and wife fertility gods.

Perhaps we can get an idea of what these places looked like by considering the churches and churchyards so common in Britain. Inside the church are sometimes buried notable people and especially clergy, sometimes with a statue; but outside where the rest are buried there are a variety of pillars, stone slabs and wooden poles bearing inscriptions often conveying the unscriptural doctrines of the apostasy, and sometimes depicting the madonna who is worshipped as a female "god" by the Catholic Church. These are the modern-day high places. When Josiah came to them he destroyed the buildings, crushed the stone slabs and pillars to powder, burned the wooden poles and dug up the skeletons of the false priests and prophets which were venerated at those sites. It is hard to imagine that the modern high places will survive the coming of the Lord Jesus Christ. And although we may appreciate the architecture of the buildings, let us beware of any sense of spiritual affinity with the religious systems which created them and the blasphemy of their teachings. In the sight of God they are part of the "abominations of the earth" which were spawned by the "mother of harlots" (Revelation 17:5). We should learn the lesson the Lord taught his disciples when he described the scribes and Pharisees who had a pretence of righteousness as "like unto whited sepulchres, which indeed appear beautiful outward, but are within full of dead men's bones ..." (Matthew 23:27).

"The zeal of thine house hath eaten me up"

We have no mandate from the Lord to do anything to the symbols of the apostasy other than witness to the Truth, but Josiah as king had that power from God and he used it wisely. His contemporaries may not have agreed with this judgement. To destroy places of worship, even those of a different religion, is considered to be sacrilege by many. But look what had happened throughout the history of Judah. Discarded images and altars had been retrieved and repositioned in the house of God; and partly destroyed high places had been restored. Josiah was not going to allow that to happen after his reforms and therefore he carried out the most complete cleansing the land had seen.

The record of 2 Kings 23 builds up the momentum of Josiah's work. The first four verses begin with the expression, "And the king ...", and so draw attention to the source of the edicts and the reforming energy. In verses 5-14 we are given a detailed list of acts beginning with the expression, "And he ..." This occurs seven times. Once started the king could not cease until he had accomplished his mission. And this zeal comes to the fore in verse 12 which refers to the destruction of the altars his grandfather had placed in the temple: "And the altars ... did the king beat down, and brake them down from thence, and cast the dust of them into the brook Kidron." The AV margin gives an interesting alternative rendering of the phrase "brake them down from thence", as "ran from thence". Strong gives the Hebrew word as *ruwts,* 'to run (for whatever reason, especially to rush)', and that is how it is usually translated. What we are given in the record is a very dramatic picture of Josiah filled with indignation against the trappings of idolatry. He was a man in a hurry, rushing to the side of the temple mount with the dust of the pulverised altars and casting them as refuse down the valley slopes.

The reference to Josiah running is particularly interesting in the light of Habakkuk. That prophecy was given after the rise of the Chaldeans but before the destruction of Jerusalem, which places it in the time of Josiah or his children. The first chapter speaks of the coming invasion which Josiah also knew about. Chapter 2 sees the prophet on his watchtower seeking an answer from God. The answer came, "Write the vision, and make it plain upon tables, that he may run that readeth it" (verse 2). Was the vision written specifically for Josiah? He was indeed a man running a race, eager to finish his work before the day of the Lord came. What was written had to be in large letters so that the runner could read and run at the same time. Josiah, we can be sure, had written the Word of God large on the tables of his heart and mind ever since the day when it was discovered in the temple. That Word was the inspiration and the source of his energy, "that he might perform the words of the law which were written in the book that Hilkiah the priest found in the house of the LORD" (2 Kings 23:24).

The zeal of Josiah was the spirit in which the Lord Jesus first cleansed the temple. The record in John 2 says that he "found in the temple those that sold oxen and sheep and doves, and the changers of money sitting: and when he had made a scourge of small cords, he drove them all out of the temple, and the sheep, and the oxen; and poured out the changers' money, and overthrew the tables ... And his disciples remembered that it was written, The zeal of thine house hath eaten me up" (verses 14-17). The Lord Jesus always did his Father's will and therefore we must see in the event the righteous indignation of God operating in the action of the Son. It is what Josiah had done when he removed the horses dedicated to the sun and cast out the vessels of idolatry.

The Lord Jesus must surely have been mindful of the parallels. When he returned to Jerusalem just before the final passover he came to the Mount of Olives where the people began to acclaim him saying, "Blessed be the King that cometh in the name of the Lord" (Luke 19:38). The Pharisees asked him to rebuke the crowd but the Lord replied, "If these should hold their peace, the stones would immediately cry out" (verse 40). He took these words from Habakkuk 2:11, "for the stone shall cry out of the wall, and the beam out of the timber shall answer it". The context is wonderfully appropriate. Habakkuk is rebuking the people with a series of "woes". In verse 9 he says, "Woe to him that coveteth an evil covetousness to his house"; verse 11 seems to be saying that the very fabric of the buildings which they erected with profits of extortion would witness against them. If the people were silent before the authority of Christ, then the very stones of Jerusalem would speak of it. And this is indeed what happened. As one stone after another was torn down by the Romans witness was given to the true identity of Jesus.

The Lord anticipated this terrible day when he looked across the Kidron valley to the temple. Standing near the place where Solomon had built the high places which Josiah had destroyed, he "beheld the city, and wept over it, saying, If thou hadst known, even thou, at least in this thy day, the things which belong unto thy peace! but now they are hid from thine eyes. For the days shall come upon thee, that thine enemies shall cast a trench about thee ... and they shall not leave in thee one stone upon another; because thou knewest not *the time of thy visitation*" (Luke 19:41-44). And then he went into the temple and cleansed it. The zeal of Josiah was unable to save Jerusalem because the hearts of the people were not touched by the Word of God. Jeremiah says, "Were they ashamed when they had committed abomination? they were not at all ashamed, neither could they blush: therefore shall they fall among them that fall: in the time of their *visitation* they shall be cast down" (8:12). When all this flooded into the mind of the Lord he wept. As we stand on the eve of an even greater day of the Lord may we learn the lesson of Josiah and follow his example, "and let us run with patience the race that is set before us".

12

THE GREAT PASSOVER

ONCE the cleansing was finished, Josiah again demonstrated his positive attitude to the things of the Truth, "saying, Keep the passover unto the LORD your God, as it is written in the book of this covenant" (2 Kings 23:21). The record of the passover which Josiah referred to was in Deuteronomy 16. In distinction to the record in Exodus 12, the original passover, this record instructed Israel what to do once they arrived in the land of promise. They were commanded to observe the instructions carefully (verse 1). The passover lambs must be taken to the only place where the Lord would allow them to be slain. The lambs were to be killed "at even, at the going down of the sun". Furthermore, the whole lamb was to be consumed before daybreak: "Neither shall there anything of the flesh, which thou sacrificest the first day at even, remain all night until the morning" (verse 4). The account ends with the command, "and thou shalt turn in the morning, and go unto thy tents". These instructions focus on the timing of events and underline the sense of "haste" with which Israel had to accomplish the feast. It could not start before evening but it had to be finished before daybreak. As soon as the sun was up they had to make their way back to their temporary dwellings. As they made their way home, their minds, tired and excited, should have been full of thankfulness; their very circumstances re-enacted the journey which their forefathers had taken out of Egypt.

As Josiah contemplated the words of the Law which he had discovered it would have become clear that there was much to be accomplished on passover night. The way in which he responded is recorded in some detail in 2 Chronicles 35.

99

2 Chronicles 35:1 specifies that "Josiah kept a passover unto the LORD in Jerusalem: and they killed the passover on the fourteenth day of the first month". Jerusalem was "the place" which is mentioned three times in Deuteronomy 16. The fourteenth day of the first month was exactly the right time to slay the lambs. This passover contrasts with the equally faithful but less orthodox obedience of Hezekiah who celebrated the passover by force of circumstances in the second month (see 2 Chronicles 30:2). The scripture record draws attention to the punctilious way in which Josiah attended to the detail of the Word of God. But let us be very clear that Josiah's motivation was not a Pharisaical observance of the ritual and ceremony of law as a means of salvation. Josiah kept the passover "unto the LORD" out of a response of love, for he "turned to the LORD with all his heart, and with all his soul, and with all his might, according to all the law of Moses" (2 Kings 23:25).

Encouraging the Workers

The first practical thing Josiah had to do to keep the passover was to ensure that the priests were properly organised: "And he set the priests in their charges, and encouraged them to the service of the house of the LORD" (2 Chronicles 35:2). The idea of the king encouraging the priests is reminiscent of the way Hezekiah carried out his reformation. Hezekiah had "commanded the people that dwelt in Jerusalem to give the portion of the priests and the Levites, that they might be encouraged in the law of the LORD" (31:4). It also says that "Hezekiah spake comfortably (AV margin, 'to the heart') unto all the Levites that taught the good knowledge of the LORD" (30:22). So Hezekiah's kindly encouragement to the Levites was to enable them to study and expound the Word of God. Josiah's encouragement to the priests was directed to their "service of the house of the LORD", but mention is also made of the Levites who are described as "the Levites that taught all Israel", once again indicating the importance placed by Josiah as well as Hezekiah on the Word of God. And of course the Word and work should always go together. It is the Word of God alone which can inform us about how to serve God acceptably, and is the

God-given power to enable us to perform that service, so that we are not hearers only.

There is a lesson for us in the approach of these kings of Judah. Like Hezekiah and Josiah we too should develop a spirit of encouragement in ecclesial life. Bible students need to encourage others to undertake their own personal study, and should take an interest in their discoveries – even if the fruits of their researches have been discovered many times before and are well known to us! And when we speak from the Word let us not forget that the Scriptures have not been given to us just to point out faults, but "that we through patience and comfort of the scriptures might have hope" (Romans 15:4).

Next, Josiah turned to the Levites that "were holy unto the LORD", and told them to "put the holy ark in the house which Solomon the son of David king of Israel did build; it shall not be a burden upon your shoulders: serve now the LORD your God, and his people Israel" (2 Chronicles 35:3). The Levites concerned were clearly faithful men, distinguished by the dual description as being teachers of Israel and "holy unto the LORD". Had these men been among those who responded to the reformation of Josiah? Or could they have been a cohort of faithful Levites who had not followed the ways of Manasseh and Amon?

Related to this is the intriguing question of when and why the ark had been removed from the temple. A very reasonable suggestion has been put forward by Brother Tom Barling in his series on Jeremiah,* that the ark had been removed whilst the temple renovations were being undertaken, and that it might have been when the ark was being removed that the Scroll of the Law was discovered. Perhaps a less plausible explanation is that faithful Levites had removed the ark to prevent it from being desecrated in the times of Manasseh and Amon. But whenever the ark had been removed it would appear that the Levites had carried it throughout its sojourn. There must have been a rota of Levites who took it in turns to hold upon their shoulders the symbol of God's presence amongst the nation. It would have been a very literal

---

* See *The Christadelphian*, May 1994, page 181.

example of holding fast the profession of hope without wavering (Hebrews 10:23, RV).

Attention is drawn to the relevance of Jeremiah 3:16,17 to this incident by Brother Tom Barling.* The target for Jeremiah is the northern remnant of Israel living in the area where Josiah had extended his cleansing. Jeremiah says, "And it shall come to pass ... they shall say no more, The ark of the covenant of the LORD: neither shall it come to mind: neither shall they remember it; neither shall they visit it; neither shall that be done any more". Is the reference to visiting the ark telling us that during the ark's temporary sojourn outside the temple, the Levites "that taught all Israel" had actually carried the ark into the northern territory as they went about teaching the people during the reformation of Josiah? The ark certainly would have been a source of intense curiosity and would have attracted the crowds. Jeremiah is explaining to this audience that the time would come when they would gladly do without the ark because the Law of the Lord would go forth from Zion where a greater King would sit on Josiah's throne (verse 17).

Preparing the Passover

The Levites were exhorted by Josiah to "prepare". The repetition of this word seven times in this section of 2 Chronicles 35 emphasises a key theme of the chapter.

First of all the Levites were told: "Prepare yourselves by the houses of your fathers, after your courses, according to the writing of David king of Israel, and according to the writing of Solomon his son". The double reference to the "writings" of David and Solomon shows that Josiah did not only study Deuteronomy but he also paid close attention to the other Scriptures at his disposal. They were then told to "stand in the holy place according to the divisions of the families (margin, 'house') of the fathers of your brethren (margin, 'the sons of') the people, and after the division of the families of the Levites" (verse 5).

This complicated instruction would seem to be referring back to the original passover command that every man

---

* See "The Ministry of Jeremiah (Chapter 3) – The Ark of the Covenant", *The Christadelphian*, October 1993, page 379.

was to take a lamb "according to the house of their fathers, a lamb for a house" (Exodus 12:3). The immense logistical problem of slaying so many lambs for so many families would require precise organisation. Heads of families would have to line up in orderly fashion and it seems that the families of Levites were assigned to minister to pre-allocated groups of families from the other tribes. Then the lambs were to be killed. The record continues by saying that the Levites were to sanctify themselves (perhaps a reference to the need to wash after slaying the lamb), and then they were to "prepare" for their brethren so that they might "do according to the word of the LORD by the hand of Moses" (2 Chronicles 35:6). This would involve the dressing of the lamb and assisting with the roasting of it so that it could be eaten and any remnants burned that same night.

An Example to Follow

Well over thirty thousand lambs were to be slain that night, as well as more than three thousand bullocks as other offerings. That would indicate perhaps at least half a million people participating in the passover meal. What is quite remarkable is that most of these animals were provided by Josiah himself. Verse 7 speaks of "all that were present" who were included in his generosity. Josiah's example prompted the princes and the senior Levites also to contribute willingly (see verses 8,9). The example of the king drew a similar if lesser response from others. And this is what is expected of us as well: "For even hereunto were ye called: because Christ also suffered for us, leaving us an example, that ye should follow his steps" (1 Peter 2:21). He gave himself willingly, which is the reason we should present our bodies as living sacrifices (Romans 12:1).

"So the service was prepared, and the priests stood in their place, and the Levites in their courses, according to the king's commandment. And they killed the passover, and the priests sprinkled the blood from their hands, and the Levites flayed them. And they removed the burnt offerings, that they might give according to the divisions of the families of the people, to offer unto the LORD, as it is written in the book of Moses. And so did they with the oxen." (2 Chronicles 35:10-12) "Removing" the burnt offerings suggests perhaps that these animals were set to one side to make room and time for the passover ceremony. But once the lambs had been killed and were being roasted the priests were busy offering up these burnt offerings (verse 14). Reference is also made to other offerings which were "sod" in pots. These must have been peace offerings (anything but roasting was forbidden in relation to the passover lambs). So much was there to do that the priests had to run to keep up with the schedule. Verse 13 says, "And they roasted the passover ... but the other holy offerings sod they in pots ... and divided them (margin, 'made them run') speedily among all the people".

The picture of hectic though orderly activity matches the scene referred to in the previous chapter when Josiah ran to cast the dust of idolatry over the side of the Kidron valley (2 Kings 23:12). Not only Josiah now but the priests as well were driven on by zeal to accomplish the Word of God. Here again we can see the example of the king rubbing off on those he encouraged. And indeed they were running a race against time. The priests had no time even to prepare their own passover meal. Referring to the work which the Levites carried out, the record says, "And afterward they made ready (RV, 'prepared') for themselves, and for the priests: because the priests the sons of Aaron were busied in offering burnt offerings and the fat until night; therefore the Levites prepared for themselves, and for the priests the sons of Aaron" (2 Chronicles 35:14). And not only did the Levites do this for the priests but they also looked after the needs of their brethren, the singers and the porters who could not leave their posts. The Levites also "prepared for them" (verse 15). Once again the Levites are a spiritual picture of ecclesial life, for the saints are also exhorted: "Bear ye one another's burdens, and so fulfil the law of Christ" (Galatians 6:2).

By the time we reach the concluding verse of this section of 2 Chronicles 35 we shall surely have appreciated the pace and urgency of events as priest and

Levite hastily worked on behalf of the people; and we can feel the note of intense satisfaction in verse 16: "So the service of the LORD was prepared the same day."

The Lord's Passover

So much of these events reminds us of the work of the Lord Jesus Christ. Like Josiah, the Lord provided the passover lamb – himself: "Christ our passover is sacrificed for us" (1 Corinthians 5:7). We have been saved by the "sprinkling of the blood of Jesus Christ" who was "a lamb without blemish and without spot" (1 Peter 1:2,19). We are on an exodus journey out of the slavery of sin, described by Peter as "the time of your sojourning" (verse 17). We, therefore, need to apply the same spirit of readiness and service which characterised the first passover and the great passover of Josiah. Peter says, "Wherefore gird up the loins of your mind" (verse 13), recalling Exodus 12:11.

The emphasis we find in 2 Chronicles 35 on the "preparation" of the passover, which was essential for the success of the event, was also evident in the Lord's passover. The Lord instructed Peter and John, saying, "Go and *prepare* us the passover, that we may eat" (Luke 22:8). They responded with the question, "Where wilt thou that we go and prepare, that *thou* mayest eat the passover?" (Mark 14:12). They were to follow a man bearing a pitcher of water and would find "a large upper room furnished and prepared" (verse 15). The disciples would indeed "make ready" the meal but their Master had it all under control without them realising it. When the disciples had asked initially they had not presumed to join Jesus in the meal. They asked, "Where wilt thou that we go and prepare, that *thou* mayest eat"; but the Lord's reply included them as part of his household: "There make ready *for us*", indicating that despite their weaknesses he would not be ashamed to call them brethren. What an encouragement this King gives to his servants!

In the upper room, quite astonishingly perhaps to us, the disciples began to argue about which of them was the greatest. The answer the Lord gave to them emphasised the greatness of serving, "For whether is greater, he that sitteth at meat, or he that serveth? is not he that sitteth at meat? but I am among you as he that serveth" (Luke

105

22:27). This was something that could been seen in the passover of Josiah. The priests, and particularly the Levites, who would surely have been counted "greater" than the people coming to the temple to partake of the feast, spent their time in service even to the point that the priests, the singers and the porters had no time to prepare their own meals.

That last supper was but a type of the true passover which was to follow. So much had to be accomplished that night. There was intense activity in the ranks of the literal priests and Levites, but this time not of the sort which had graced the passover of Josiah. Now the priests and Levites ran around to bring about the crucifixion of the Lord. Unknowingly they were making preparations to kill the greatest Passover Lamb of all!

The Leaven of Malice and Wickedness

The passover of Josiah, with so many people present, and so thoroughly scriptural, with priest and Levite on top of their form, and the choral accompaniment singing the Psalms of David, Asaph, Heman and Jeduthun (2 Chronicles 35:15), was the greatest since the days of Samuel. We cannot imagine then that Josiah would have overlooked the passover instruction about leaven.

In the Exodus record Israel were commanded on the first day of the feast of unleavened bread to "put away leaven out of your houses" (Exodus 12:15). The instruction is repeated in different words in verse 19: "There shall be no leaven found in your houses", and again in 13:7: "There shall no leavened bread be seen with thee, neither shall there be leaven seen with thee in all thy quarters." In the Deuteronomy 16 record the latter instruction is repeated: "And there shall be no leavened bread seen with thee in all thy coast" (verse 4). The spiritual significance of leaven is explained by the Apostle Paul when he says to the Corinthians, "Purge out therefore the old leaven, that ye may be a new lump, as ye are unleavened" (1 Corinthians 5:7). The old leaven was the example of fornication in the ecclesia which was in danger of corrupting the whole ecclesia. It was the old way of life out of which the Corinthians had been redeemed. If this point is applied to Israel at passover, the leaven would have represented the influences of Egypt which had to be set aside before Israel could become the people of God. But Paul adds another application. If there was an "old" leaven, there was also a new leaven they should identify and exclude from their ecclesial house: "Therefore let us keep the feast, not with the old leaven, neither with the leaven of malice and wickedness; but with the unleavened bread of sincerity and truth" (verse 8). The "new" leaven was the childish competitiveness and jealousies which were stunting their spiritual growth (3:3).

In Josiah's passover there is no particular mention of leaven although the nation did keep the seven-day feast of unleavened bread (2 Chronicles 35:17). But there is no doubt that Josiah, and it seems also at least the Levites as well, kept that feast in sincerity and truth. Given the reproofs of Jeremiah there must be considerable doubt about the sincerity of most of the congregation. What is also very interesting, however, is the 2 Kings 23 record which says immediately after reference to the celebration of the passover: "Moreover the workers with familiar spirits, and the wizards, and the images, and the idols, and all the abominations that were spied in the land of Judah and Jerusalem, did Josiah put away" (verse 24). These abominations represented the old leaven which Israel were commanded to "put away". The reference to that which was "spied in the land" implies a seeking out of the leaven, as both Exodus 13 and Deuteronomy 16 required: "There shall be no leavened bread seen with thee in all thy coast." The "images" mentioned were the "teraphim" or household gods. These small figurines would only be found by a thorough search of the houses. Exodus 12:15 says, "Ye shall put away leaven out of your houses", and Zephaniah prophesies, "And it shall come to pass at that time, that I will search Jerusalem with candles" (1:12), perhaps indicating a literal searching of the house of Judah for the evidences of idolatry. We would do well to follow this example, and make sure that in our own houses there are no household gods which, like leaven, can insidiously take over our lives.

13

JOSIAH AS A TYPE OF CHRIST

THE great passover of Josiah was celebrated in the eighteenth year of his reign, the same year that the book of the Law was discovered. Josiah reigned another thirteen years and yet nothing is said of this period in the records of 2 Kings and 2 Chronicles. All we find is the summary of his character. How were those thirteen years spent? It must have been a difficult time because he knew that despite his best efforts the nation could not be saved from the judgements of God. 2 Kings 23 draws attention to this sad state of things. Having defined the uniquely good reign of Josiah in verse 25, the record goes on to say, "Notwithstanding the LORD turned not from the fierceness of his great wrath, wherewith his anger was kindled against Judah, because of all the provocations that Manasseh had provoked him withal. And the LORD said, I will remove Judah also out of my sight, as I have removed Israel, and will cast off this city Jerusalem, which I have chosen, and the house of which I said, My name shall be there" (verses 26,27). Difficult as it must have been, however, it was to be no different for the Lord Jesus who knew that the nation he had been sent to save would reject him and as a consequence would be taken into captivity and lose their city and their temple.

Even if we are not given any details about those last 13 years of Josiah's life, we are given an insight into the man himself: "Now the rest of the acts of Josiah, and his goodness, according to that which was written in the law of the LORD, and his deeds, first and last, behold, they are written in the book of the kings of Israel and Judah" (2 Chronicles 35:26,27). "Goodness" is the word *chesed*, meaning 'lovingkindness', the word which is used so many times in relation to the character of God. *Chesed* is the one attribute of the character of Yahweh revealed in Exodus 34:6,7 which is repeated, so emphasising its importance.

There, it says that the Lord is "abundant in goodness (*chesed*) and truth, keeping mercy (*chesed*) for thousands". The New Testament translation of the expression "goodness and truth" is to be found in John 1:14 where we are told that the Lord Jesus Christ in manifesting the glory of the Father was "full of grace and truth". In the New Testament therefore the word "grace" stands for the "lovingkindness" (*chesed*) of God. Like Hezekiah before him (2 Chronicles 32:32), Josiah was a man who manifested the character of his God, not just in breaking down idols but also in his words of encouragement and acts of kindness, so much so that it is this characteristic which is mentioned in his obituary. In this respect also Josiah was a type of Christ.

"The cause of the poor and needy"

Jeremiah gives us more of an insight into the character of Josiah when he contrasts the king with the character of his sons who later ascended the throne. In 22:16, Jeremiah says of Josiah: "He judged the cause of the poor and needy; then it was well with him: was not this to know me? saith the LORD". Remember how Josiah was concerned that all the people "from the smallest even unto the greatest" should have the benefits of entering into covenant relationship with God, and how in providing the passover lambs for the people, the poor and needy were catered for by the grace of this king.

Where had Josiah learned this approach to kingship? From the Law which he had discovered. In Deuteronomy 10:17,18, Moses says, "For the LORD your God is God of gods, and Lord of lords, a great God, a mighty, and a terrible, which regardeth not persons, nor taketh reward: he doth execute the judgment of the fatherless and widow, and loveth the stranger, in giving him food and raiment". But how did God exercise this impartial lovingkindness to the poor and needy? Surely it was in large measure through the Law itself. If the people kept the Law then the poor and the needy would be cared for. It was the Lord's intention that His people would be the means by which His love and care would be ministered. For instance, tithes were to be laid up in the cities: "And the Levite (because he hath no part nor inheritance with thee), and

109

the stranger, and the fatherless, and the widow, which are within thy gates, shall come, and shall eat and be satisfied" (Deuteronomy 14:29). If a man fell on hard times then the Law commanded his neighbours to be generous to him: "Thou shalt not harden thine heart, nor shut thine hand from thy poor brother: but thou shalt open thine hand wide unto him, and shalt surely lend him sufficient for his need, in that which he wanteth" (15:7,8). The poor and needy were to be invited to join in the celebration of the feast of weeks (16:11) and tabernacles (verse 14). Farmers were not allowed to glean their own fields, but were to leave the remnant for the stranger, fatherless and widow (24:21).

Knowing the Lord

As a man of the Book, Josiah sought to implement the spirit of these laws. In so doing he came to "know" the Lord whom he served – "Was not this to know me?" Jeremiah amplifies this point: "Thus saith the LORD, Let not the wise man glory in his wisdom, neither let the mighty man glory in his might, let not the rich man glory in his riches: but let him that glorieth glory in this, that he understandeth and knoweth me, that I am the LORD which exerciseth lovingkindness, judgment, and righteousness in the earth: for in these things I delight, saith the LORD" (9:23,24). The idea of knowing the Lord by following the commandments of God is expounded in 1 John. In his epistle John uses two different Greek words which are translated "to know". One word means a full understanding, an intellectual knowledge – we "know that". But the other word means to know by experience as in knowing a person. It is this second word, knowing by experience, which is used in the following verses: "And hereby we do *know* that we *know* him; if we keep his commandments. He that saith, I *know* him, and keepeth not his commandments, is a liar, and the truth is not in him. But whoso keepeth his word, in him verily is the love of God perfected: hereby *know* we that we are in him" (1 John 2:3-5). God's commandments express His character and therefore His love and mercy. As we carry out those commands we fulfil God's intention and therefore "the love of God", which is implicit in the command, is "perfected" or

110

completed. By following the commandment we come to understand and appreciate that character, aligning our thoughts with His. We come to know by experience the character of God revealed in His Word: "He that loveth not knoweth not God; for God is love" (1 John 4:8).

John gives us a practical example of this principle: "Hereby perceive (know by experience) we the love of God, because he laid down his life for us: and we ought to lay down our lives for the brethren. But whoso hath this world's good, and seeth his brother have need, and shutteth up his bowels of compassion from him, how dwelleth the love of God in him?" (1 John 3:16,17). This example expresses the spirit of Deuteronomy 15 to which we have already referred. The Israelite was to open his hand wide to his needy brother. But opening the hand can only happen when we have first opened our hearts in compassion. The opposite is to shut up our bowels of compassion and consequently keep our hands tightly clenched around our resources.

The links between Josiah (as presented in Jeremiah 22) and 1 John help us understand the unexpected last verse of the epistle: "Little children, keep yourselves from idols." This is the first time John has mentioned idols, but in relation to Josiah we can see the relevance. It was idolatry which in Josiah's time had replaced the Truth, and as a consequence the character of God was not being manifested in the nation. Removing idols is essential if we are to concentrate our minds and energies on knowing the Lord.

The words of Jeremiah 9:23,24 are further developed by the Apostle Paul. In his epistle to the ecclesia at Corinth he reminds them that "the world by wisdom knew not God" (1 Corinthians 1:21). He then goes on to draw exhortation from Jeremiah 9: "Ye see your calling, brethren, how that not many wise men after the flesh, not many mighty, not many noble, are called ... that no flesh should glory in his presence ... that according as it is written, He that glorieth, let him glory in the Lord" (verses 26-31). Here it is not just the last verse which comes from Jeremiah 9. The references to the wise, mighty and the noble parallel the wise, mighty and rich of

Jeremiah 9:23. The Corinthians were to understand that they were the "poor and needy" who had been the recipients of the lovingkindness of the "King", for God had made the Lord Jesus their (and our) "wisdom and righteousness, and sanctification, and redemption" (1 Corinthians 1:30). The Father had delighted to show His *chesed* character to the Corinthians through the Gospel, and they who had come to know God through the Lord Jesus Christ were now to show the same lovingkindness to one another (see 1 Corinthians 13).

The background to Jeremiah 9 is the reign of Josiah who manifestly knew God. Did Paul have Josiah ('founded of Yah') in mind when he went on to tell the Corinthians: "According to the grace of God which is given unto me, as a wise masterbuilder, I have laid *the foundation*, and another buildeth thereon. But let every man take heed how he buildeth thereupon. For other foundation can no man lay than that is laid, which is Jesus Christ" (1 Corinthians 3:10,11)?

"After all this"

The end of Josiah's reign came when he was just 39 years old. It seems on the natural plane to be a premature end, but the Scripture record indicates that Josiah was only taken away when he had finished his work. The introduction to the final stages of his reign is introduced in this way: "After all this, when Josiah had prepared the temple, Necho king of Egypt came up ..." (2 Chronicles 35:20). Is "the house" referred to in this passage (verse 21) the actual temple building? If it was, Josiah's legacy would not last very long. Only 40 or so years later that temple was completely destroyed. In view of the meaning of Josiah's name it must be significant that the end of his life should come "when he prepared the house". In 2 Chronicles 35, the word "prepare" occurs eight times. The first seven occurrences have to do with preparing the priests and Levites, the people, the service, and the passover itself. The use of the word draws attention to the diligence of Josiah so that the passover could be celebrated that day. The eighth occurrence of the word may suggest that a new and different type of work was in preparation after passover.

112

The house that Josiah was preparing during the last 13 years of his life was a spiritual house. During that period a generation of faithful disciples was nurtured. Some would be very young, such as Daniel, Hananiah, Mishael and Azariah, and Ezekiel the prophet. It is interesting to note that the prophecy of Ezekiel opens "in the thirtieth year", which was said to be the fifth year of Jehoiachin's captivity, and whatever the significance of the 30th year (perhaps Ezekiel's age at the time) this time period began in the 26th year of Josiah, the year the book of the Law was found – so marking out a new era in the history of God's people. Where else than under the tutelage of Josiah did Daniel and his friends get such strength of character and faithfulness? And here also is a parallel with the work of the Lord Jesus Christ who himself was the foundation of the house of God and who also told his disciples, "In my Father's house are many abiding-places (RV margin) ... I go to prepare a place for you" (John 14:2).

The circumstances of the death of Josiah illustrate, as do all types, that no one could perfectly foreshadow the Lord Jesus. It seems clear that Josiah should not have gone out to fight against Pharaoh-Necho. Necho was on his way to Carchemish to support the Assyrians against the resurgent Babylonians. Pharaoh's rebuff to Josiah who came against him in battle included the words, "Forbear thee from meddling with God"; and the Chronicles account adds, "Nevertheless Josiah would not turn his face from him ... and hearkened not unto the words of Necho from the mouth of God" (2 Chronicles 35:22). It was an aberration on the part of Josiah. What was he thinking of? And yet his death was in accordance with the promise of God to take Josiah away before he could see the destruction which was to come on Jerusalem. At the battle of Megiddo he was hit by an arrow and died on his way back to Jerusalem.

The news of the death of that lovely man must have shattered Jeremiah and the other members of the faithful remnant: "And Jeremiah lamented for Josiah: and all the singing men and the singing women spake of Josiah in their lamentations to this day, and made them an ordinance in Israel: and, behold, they are written in the

113

lamentations" (2 Chronicles 35:25). The book we know as Lamentations does not have any direct references to Josiah but there are echoes of the circumstances of his death. For example, Lamentations 2 says, "He hath cut off in his fierce anger ... he hath drawn back his right hand before the enemy ... he hath bent his bow like an enemy" (verses 3,4). Certainly the arrow that struck Josiah was not intended for the king, because he had disguised himself. The Egyptians would not have known they were shooting at him. It was God's arrow that struck him and how appropriate the words of Lamentations 3:12,13 would be of Josiah: "He hath bent his bow, and set me as a mark for the arrow. He hath caused the arrows of his quiver to enter into my reins." Are these the thoughts of Josiah as he lay dying in his chariot, now taken up by Jeremiah to epitomise the state of the nation?

Perhaps there is another reflection on the life of Josiah in the words of Lamentations 3:27: "It is good for a man that he bear the yoke in his youth." At the tender age of 8 Josiah came to the throne. When he was just 16 years old he began to seek after the God of David his father. At 20 he took up the responsibility of cleansing the land from idolatry. He was rewarded with the discovery of the book of the Law which gave a new strength to his reforms. He humbled himself before the Word of God and turned to Him with all his heart, and soul and strength. He did not deviate from the narrow way and was known not just for zeal but also for his lovingkindness. Certainly it was good that this man took up the yoke in his youth so that he might be an inspiration for us all to follow more diligently the Lord Jesus whom he prefigured.

The nation lamented for Josiah, even though their hearts were not in the reforms of their king. Nevertheless, they saw something to admire in Josiah, and surely life under a just and merciful king must have been better than in the days of Manasseh and Amon. The sorrow of the nation at that time is used by the prophet Zechariah to portray how the nation will respond when they come to know that Jesus, whom they crucified, is their King. But in contrast to Josiah's day, the nation then will have had their hearts opened and will enter into the new covenant willingly: "And I will pour upon the house of David, and upon the inhabitants of Jerusalem, the spirit of grace and of supplications: and they shall look upon me whom they have pierced, and they shall mourn for him, as one mourneth for his only son, and shall be in bitterness for him, as one that is in bitterness for his firstborn. In that day shall there be a great mourning in Jerusalem, as the mourning of Hadadrimmon in the valley of Megiddon" (Zechariah 12:10,11).

The Word of God will be written in their hearts as they appreciate through experience the lovingkindness which has been shown to them. And as a result Zechariah describes a reformation greater even than that of Josiah: "In that day there shall be a fountain opened to the house of David and to the inhabitants of Jerusalem for sin and for uncleanness ... I will cut off the names of the idols out of the land, and they shall no more be remembered: and also I will cause the prophets and the unclean spirit to pass out of the land" (13:1,2). As Josiah stands next to the Lord Jesus in that day and admires the King who could remove idols from the heart of his people, how thankful he will be that he took up the yoke in his youth.

JOSIAH AS A TYPE OF CHRIST		
JOSIAH		*CHRIST*
1 Kings 13:2	Came by Prophecy	Luke 1:32
2 Chronicles 34:3	Sought God in his Youth	Luke 2:49
2 Chronicles 34:8	Cleansed Temple (1st)	John 2:13-16
2 Kings 23:2	Revealed the Word	John 1:14
2 Chronicles 34:6	Went about doing Good	Acts 10:38
2 Chronicles 34:33	Sought Lost Sheep of Israel	Luke 15
2 Kings 23	Condemned Idolatry	Matthew 23
2 Kings 23:4	Cleansed the Temple (2nd)	Mark 11:15-17
2 Kings 22:17	Impending Disaster Foretold	Mark 13
2 Chronicles 35:20	Prepared House	John 14:2
2 Chronicles 35:1	Prepared Passover	Mark 14:15
2 Chronicles 35:7	Provided the Passover Lamb	1 Corinthians 5:7
2 Kings 23:2	Instituted a New Covenant	Mark 14:24
2 Kings 23:25	Unique Character	John 1:14

14

JOSIAH'S CHILDREN CHOOSE DEATH!

THE death of Josiah left the kingdom of Judah in the hands of his sons and grandson for the last forty years of its existence before the Babylonians destroyed the city of David and the house of God. That last generation was a terrible disappointment after the splendid efforts of Josiah. Each of the kings is dismissed in the Scripture record as being evil. No good thing is said of them. Nevertheless, during that period a faithful remnant survived and through the captivity in Babylon they developed into a people who would never again worship idols of wood and stone. Foremost among these were Daniel, Hananiah, Mishael and Azariah. This was the true legacy of Josiah.

When we put these historical facts together, what becomes apparent is that in the "ecclesia" in Jerusalem after the death of Josiah there was a group of young people, each surrounded by the same influences for good and evil, each able to choose how they would respond, some choosing for good and others for evil. The book of the Law had presented Israel on their entry into the land with just such a choice. There Moses said to the nation:

> "I call heaven and earth to record this day against you, that I have set before you life and death, blessing and cursing: therefore choose life, that both thou and thy seed may live: that thou mayest love the LORD thy God, and that thou mayest obey his voice, and that thou mayest cleave unto him: for he is thy life, and the length of thy days: that thou mayest dwell in the land which the LORD sware unto thy fathers, to Abraham, to Isaac, and to Jacob, to give them."   (Deuteronomy 30:19,20)

Now this choice was being made for the last time. The book of Deuteronomy had been newly discovered, so the appeal to Josiah's children should have been as fresh to them as it was to Joshua and his generation. But they were, with few exceptions, to choose evil and all the curses in that book would come upon them.

Here are powerful lessons for our generation. Our young people today are under greater pressure than ever before to conform to a world heading swiftly towards judgement. It may seem at times that ecclesial decay is an inevitable part of this trend. But it need not be so. Despite the inevitability of the Babylonian invasion in the days of Josiah's children a faithful remnant did survive, their characters developed in the maelstrom of that society. The same can be true today. But there are also serious warnings. Josiah was a faithful and impressive rôle model for his sons, surely, and yet each of them turned against the example their father had set. There was no inheriting of his faith, and Josiah's sons were not to be saved because of who their father was. And the same will be true at the judgement seat of Christ. Our children who have reached the age of responsibility will have to give account personally for the way they have chosen to respond to the influences bearing upon them. The principle is very clearly stated by Ezekiel who himself grew up in this same period and environment: "The soul that sinneth, it shall die" (Ezekiel 18:4).

Jehoahaz – "He did that which was evil"
The first of Josiah's sons to ascend the throne was Jehoahaz and he was 23 years old. His brother Jehoiakim was 25 years old when he took over just three months later. That makes Jehoiakim two years older than his brother Jehoahaz who was preferred to him. Eleven years later the third brother, Zedekiah, came to the throne at the age of 21. No other brothers are mentioned in the historical records, but, in 1 Chronicles 3:15 a different set of names appears: "And the sons of Josiah were, the firstborn Johanan, the second Jehoiakim, the third Zedekiah, the fourth Shallum." It has been suggested that the firstborn Johanan died before Josiah and therefore did not ascend to the throne. Shallum does not appear in the historical record and it is suggested that this was just another name for Jehoahaz. Certainly this whole section of Scripture is notable for the number of name changes.

The problem with this explanation is the order of the sons. In 2 Kings 23,24 the age order is Jehoiakim, Jehoahaz then Zedekiah. If Shallum is Jehoahaz then he should be the second (or third) not the fourth. An explanation which harmonises the two apparently contradictory passages is that the word "firstborn" in 1 Chronicles 3:15 is not used in the literal sense of the first son to be born, but in the sense of the one who assumed the rôle of firstborn by succeeding his father. An example of this usage is found in regard to the sons of Joseph. Manasseh was the actual firstborn (Genesis 48:14) but the Lord says in Jeremiah 31:9, "Ephraim is my firstborn". Johanan would then be another name for Jehoahaz and the Shallum of 1 Chronicles 3:15 the fourth and youngest son who never took the throne. The only problem for this explanation is that in Jeremiah 22 the name "Shallum" is applied to Jehoahaz who was taken captive into Egypt. Is it possible that he took on the name of his youngest brother who had died?

Jehoahaz was made king after Josiah's death when he was twenty-three years old and therefore he must have been only nine or ten when the Law was discovered and the great reformation took place. He would be able to recall the great passover and the zeal with which his father had cleansed the land. He had a further thirteen years under the guidance of Josiah and yet in his short reign of three months he earned an unenviable reputation in Scripture: "And he did that which was evil in the sight of the LORD, according to all that his fathers had done" (2 Kings 23:32). The reference to "his fathers" must be ironic since he certainly did not do as his own father had done. Instead he must have chosen as his rôle model his grandfather Amon or his great-grandfather Manasseh before he repented.

Jehoahaz was deposed from the throne by Pharaoh-Necho, who "put him in bands at Riblah in the land of Hamath, that he might not reign in Jerusalem; and put the land to a tribute of an hundred talents of silver, and a talent of gold" (verse 33). If this Jehoahaz is the Shallum of Jeremiah 22, as seems likely, then Jeremiah in that chapter was informing the people that there was no use hoping for his return. The man they had preferred to his older brother was not coming back: "He shall not return thither any more: but he shall die in the place whither they have led him captive, and shall see this land no more" (verses 11,12).

It is hard to understand how a son could go so wrong so quickly. Some have argued that perhaps Josiah was so busy with the work of the Truth that he neglected his family, and that certainly can happen. But when we think just how concerned Josiah was to follow the newly discovered Word of God, it hardly seems credible that he would not have given due attention to the instructions in Deuteronomy to bring up his sons in the way of the Lord to the best of his ability. Deuteronomy 6:5 is the verse which summarises the life of Josiah. There was no king before or since who "turned to the LORD" with all his heart, soul and might. Verse 7 then goes on to instruct Israel to teach that Word at every opportunity to their children: "And thou shalt teach them diligently unto thy children, and shalt talk of them when thou sittest in thine house, and when thou walkest by the way, and when thou liest down, and when thou risest up." Josiah did not deviate from the way of the Lord and therefore we can be sure that he did not neglect his family in this way.

Just what went wrong can perhaps be discerned when we consider Jehoahaz's brother, and that has to do with rebellion against the Word of God from his youth. But there is one other clue which yields an interesting insight into the mentality of Josiah's children. Zephaniah who prophesied in the reign of Josiah comments upon the king's children. The setting is the impending judgement upon the idolatrous worshippers in Jerusalem. He says, "And it shall come to pass in the day of the LORD's sacrifice, that I will punish the princes, and the king's children, and all such as are clothed with strange apparel" (1:8).

A Fashion not to Follow

"Strange apparel" literally means "foreign clothes". Josiah's sons had, it seems, taken up a fashion which identified them with the nations whose practices were abominable to Yahweh. We recall the "goodly Babylonish

119

garment" which Achan coveted when the spoil of Jericho was taken, a garment which brought ruin to his house. The true garment of the Israelite was to have a hem of blue cloth:

"Speak unto the children of Israel, and bid them that they make them fringes in the borders of their garments throughout their generations, and that they put upon the fringe of the borders a ribband of blue ... that ye may look upon it, and remember all the commandments of the LORD, and do them; and that ye seek not after your own heart and your own eyes, after which ye used to go a whoring." (Numbers 15:38,39)

This command applied to Jehoahaz and his brothers – "throughout their generations". As he took a step forward the ribband of blue should have reminded him of the covering over the ark representing the God of Heaven. The ark had gone before them to lead them in right ways, and so each step in life was to be taken in that spirit. By discarding such clothing for foreign attire the sons of Josiah had literally cast off the God-given memory aid to walk in the ways of the Lord and not to walk in the immoral ways of the nations.

And although we may argue that our clothing today does not in itself carry spiritual significance as did the clothes of Israel with borders of blue, and the priestly garments representing holiness, glory and beauty, we cannot ignore the fact that clothing today can have associations which the disciple of Christ should avoid. Clothing may be deliberately chosen to identify with a particular trend in ideas and values which are alien to the Hope of Israel. This includes clothing which accentuates the figure and which is designed to tempt the opposite sex "to go a whoring". (This fashion would fit very well into the worship of Asherah which Josiah so hated.) Today, advertisements encourage everyone, not just young people, to "make a statement" by their dress. Clothes may be part of self-expression which speaks of assertiveness (for "liberated" women), success and materialism (for businessmen) or rebellion against authority (in the youth culture). We need to take care that we are not literally caught up in this sort of mentality. Josiah's sons had clearly been influenced by a sinister fashion associated with idolatry and vice, and they were about to suffer the consequences. For us perhaps the daily readings take on the role of the ribband of blue to remind us constantly to walk in the way of the Lord. How easy it is to forget our high calling in Christ once we neglect to do our readings.

The section of Zephaniah we have just looked at has a very particular application to the saints because it is used by the Lord Jesus in a parable given during the last week of his ministry when the echoes of the work of Josiah were at their strongest. We have already seen many of the connections of thought between Josiah and the work of the Lord at this time. In Matthew 21 the Lord, like Josiah, cleanses the temple, and quotes a relevant passage from the times of Josiah – Jeremiah 7. He is about to institute a new covenant and celebrate a great passover, as did Josiah. In the parable of Matthew 22:1-14 the Lord weaves together Old Testament scripture, including Zephaniah 1:7,8.

Zephaniah speaks of a feast which is to be celebrated in the company of invited guests: "Hold thy peace at the presence of the Lord GOD: for the day of the LORD is at hand: for the LORD hath prepared a sacrifice, he hath bid his guests. And it shall come to pass in the day of the LORD's sacrifice, that I will punish the princes, and the king's children, and all such as are clothed with strange apparel." The feast is of course an ironic description of the destruction of Jerusalem. The invited guests are the Babylonian armies. The strange apparel is the emblem of idolatry worn by an apostate nation who now were to be justly removed from their inheritance. In the parable of the Lord Jesus another feast is described: "The kingdom of heaven is like unto a certain king, which made a marriage for his son, and sent forth his servants to call them that were bidden to the wedding: and they would not come" (Matthew 22:2,3). Others were invited: "Behold, I have prepared my dinner" (verse 4). Still they would not respond and the king "sent forth his armies, and destroyed those murderers, and burned up their city" (verse 7). Here was a clear prophecy of the destruction of Jerusalem by the Romans because the Jews would not respond to the call of the Gospel. Now the Gospel was to go forth to the Gentiles. The Lord says in the parable, "Go ye therefore into the highways, and as many as ye shall find, bid to the marriage. So those servants went out into the highways, and gathered together all as many as they found, both bad and good: and the wedding was furnished with guests" (verses 9,10).

"All that were present"

Note the use of "all as many as they found". It is a reference to the approach of Josiah when he "caused all that were present (found) in Jerusalem and Benjamin to stand" to the new covenant (2 Chronicles 34:32), and when he "gave to the people, of the flock, lambs and kids, all for the passover offerings, for all that were present (found)" (35:7).

When the king comes in to see the guests, "he saw there a man which had not on a wedding garment: and he saith unto him, Friend, how camest thou in hither not having a wedding garment? And he was speechless" (Matthew 22:11,12). That ill clothed guest was bound hand and foot and cast out into outer darkness. (We shall see that this literally happened to Jehoiakim when "they put him in ward in chains, and brought him to the king of Babylon" (Ezekiel 19:9). We can hardly miss the link to Zephaniah 1. What had been true of the sons of Josiah is now applied to the one who has responded to the call of the Gospel but whose way of life is inconsistent with that calling. Saints must "put off" as a garment "the old man with his deeds" and "put on the new man, which is renewed in knowledge after the image of him that created him" (Colossians 3:9,10). If we do not wear the garments of righteousness then we shall be considered to be clothed in "strange apparel" as far as the bridegroom is concerned when he comes. If that is the case we shall be dealt the same judgement as that of Jehoahaz and Jehoiakim. We shall lose the kingdom.

Jehoiakim – "he did that which was evil"

Pharaoh-Necho put Eliakim on the throne in place of his brother and changed his name to Jehoiakim – 'Yah has established'. The changing of this name would seem to be either a superstitious attempt to secure the king's favour with Yahweh by building the name of God into that of the king, or a politically astute move to win the respect of the people of Judah. One writer notes that all the kings after Josiah had their names changed to ones containing "Yah", and he concluded "that the custom was one effect of the reforms of Josiah". Apparently, in the Hebrew inscriptions found at Lachish dating from this time most proper names carry the same element.

Jehoiakim was faithful to Egypt and duly taxed the people to pay the tribute (2 Kings 23:35). There is a strong indication that he raised taxes in the same way as the New Testament publicans, taking more than the Egyptians required and using the rest to fill his own coffers. Jeremiah has much to say about this. In chapter 22 he says of Jehoiakim: "Woe unto him that buildeth his house by unrighteousness, and his chambers by wrong; that useth his neighbour's service without wages, and giveth him not for his work; that saith, I will build me a wide house and large chambers, and cutteth him out windows; and it is cieled with cedar, and painted with vermilion" (Jeremiah 22:13,14). It seems very likely that archaeologists have unearthed this palace which Jeremiah so condemned. At Ramat Rahel just south of Jerusalem, excavations by Aharoni from 1954-63 discovered the remains of an extensive, imposing palace with walls of ashlar blocks of similar style to Ahab's palace in Samaria, though dated to the time of Jehoiakim. One notable feature was the ornamental windows with their balustrades of miniature palmette pillars decorated with ornate capitals. That archaeologists should draw attention to the lavishness of the architecture does corroborate quite remarkably the observations of Jeremiah.

Jehoiakim certainly was going to enjoy the privileges of being king, perhaps making up for all the things his father had refused him. But Jeremiah challenges the king with the words: "Shalt thou reign, because thou closest thyself in cedar?" (verse 15). Was it living in a palace and wearing royal garments which made a man a king? Not in the sight of the Lord. The throne on which the kings of Judah sat was, if they only would realise it, the throne of the Lord over Israel (1 Chronicles 29:23). The Lord looked for the kingly qualities of seeking first the Kingdom of God and His righteousness, as Josiah had so well exemplified. So Jeremiah contrasts the thinking of Jehoiakim with that of his father:

"Did not thy father eat and drink, and do judgment and justice, and then it was well with him? He judged the cause of the poor and needy; then it was well with him: was not this to know me? saith the LORD. But thine eyes and thine heart are not but for thy covetousness, and for to shed innocent blood, and for oppression, and for violence, to do it."   (Jeremiah 22:15-17)

The responsibility of Jehoiakim was all the greater because he had been brought up in the way of the Lord. He had been just eleven years old when the Law was discovered and would have remembered perhaps even more vividly than Jehoahaz the reforming work of his father. Would we not expect a young boy at that age to have been inspired by the firm and exciting leadership his father was giving to the nation? Would we not have expected this oldest son to have modelled himself upon the king and determined to carry on the work when he in turn ascended to the throne? But that was not how Jehoiakim was to respond. His was a rebellious attitude to the good example set by his father. His dishonest, cruel, heartless and materialistic ways had not been learned from Josiah. But the potential for all of these sins of the flesh lies within each one of us. We also are always in need of the exhortation to "mortify therefore your members which are upon the earth" (Colossians 3:5), and it is always possible for those who have known the way of righteousness to "turn from the holy commandment delivered unto them" like a dog returning to its own vomit or a sow to her wallowing in the mire (2 Peter 2:21,22). But herein lay the folly of Jehoiakim. He would not listen to the Word of exhortation but, like his brothers, followed the fashion of this world.

15

JOSIAH'S SON REJECTS THE WORD OF GOD

THREE months from his father's death, Jehoiakim became king and immediately manifested all the attributes which were abominable to his father. Such a character was not developed overnight. Despite his father's example and a Godly upbringing, Jehoiakim resented the intrusion of the Word of God into his life. He made the very opposite response to that shown by his father. Through Jeremiah the Lord says: "I spake unto thee in thy prosperity; but thou saidst, I will not hear. This hath been thy manner *from thy youth*, that thou obeyedst not my voice" (Jeremiah 22:21). What a contrast with young King Josiah who from the age of 16 began to seek after the God of David, and who cherished the Word of God from the time it was rediscovered.

To "obey the voice" of the Lord was the great appeal of the book of Deuteronomy which Josiah had discovered. In that book Moses reminded the people, as they stood on the verge of entering the land of promise, that their fathers had heard the voice of God speaking from heaven in a unique manner: "Did ever people hear the voice of God speaking out of the midst of the fire, as thou hast heard, and live? ... Out of heaven he made thee to hear his voice, that he might instruct thee" (4:33,36; 5:24,26).

This response from the nation was commended by the Lord who said, "O that there were such an heart in them, that they would fear me, and keep all my commandments always, that it might be well with them, and with their children for ever" (5:29). But such reverence for the "voice of God" was completely absent from the mentality of Josiah's children. Obedience to the voice of God was the principle upon which kingship over Israel was founded. It was because Saul had refused to hear (obey) the "voice of the LORD" (1 Samuel 15:22) that the kingdom was taken away from him. And now the same thing was going to happen to Jehoiakim.

From his youth Jehoiakim rebelled against the Word of God. It is why he turned out as he did. An example of the opposite response can be seen in the case of Timothy who when he was young – "from a child" – listened to his mother and grandmother who instructed him in the Scriptures. This is why "unfeigned faith" dwelt in him as well as in Lois and Eunice. But why was it that Timothy would listen and Jehoiakim would not? How much of it was due to their upbringing? Timothy who listened to the Word had an unbelieving Gentile father, and Jehoiakim who would not listen had a father who was a giant of faith. Perhaps it was the influence of the mothers. It is certainly the case that mothers are important in the spiritual development of their children.

The names of the mothers of Josiah's children are given in Scripture, suggesting that they did have an important influence; and there is perhaps a cryptic reference to these women in Jeremiah 44, where the prophet asks the people who had escaped to Egypt after the destruction of Jerusalem: "Have ye forgotten the wickedness of ... the kings of Judah, and the wickedness of their wives ... which they have committed in the land of Judah, and in the streets of Jerusalem?" (verse 9).

The contrast between Jehoiakim and Timothy serves to highlight the rôle of mothers in the development of faithful children, but in the final analysis we shall have to conclude that the difference in response comes down eventually to the choice of the individual. Certainly, the Scriptures tell us to bring up our children in the way they should go and when they are old they will not depart from it. But it is possible that a child may refuse to yield to the Word of God, and though he may conform to his father's wishes in an outward observance he may yet in his heart resent that imposition. In this case the child never was brought successfully into the way of the Lord, for that way is a matter of receiving the Word of God into the heart. Jehoiakim's rejection of the Word of God from his youth was also prominent throughout his eleven year reign. Consider how he responded to the prophecies of Jeremiah.

Jehoiakim Rejects Jeremiah's Prophecy

The prophecy of Jeremiah 26 was set "in the beginning of the reign of Jehoiakim" (verse 1). Jeremiah was to stand in the court of the temple and challenge the people to respond. In the spirit of Deuteronomy 4, Jeremiah was told to transmit every word that was revealed to him by God – "diminish not a word" (verse 2). Perhaps "they will hearken, and turn every man from his evil way, that I may repent me of the evil, which I purpose to do unto them because of the evil of their doings" (verse 3). The message from the Lord promised destruction of Jerusalem if the nation would not respond. When the leaders heard the prophecy, they were outraged and arrested poor Jeremiah and threatened to kill him. At the trial before the princes the charges were brought by "the priests and the prophets", the men who were responsible for officiating over the corruption of society. Their case was that "this man is worthy to die; for he hath prophesied against this city, as ye have heard with your ears" (verse 11). Jeremiah's defence was to reiterate the command he had received to speak faithfully all the words of God which were revealed to him.

Surprisingly, the judges' response was favourable: "Then said the princes and all the people unto the priests and to the prophets; This man is not worthy to die: for he hath spoken to us in the name of the LORD our God" (verse 16). But bear in mind that this was only months after the death of Josiah, and his influence upon the rulers would not yet have faded completely. Amongst the judges were "certain of the elders of the land" who drew attention to the way in which king Hezekiah and the nation had responded to the prophecy of Micah, when Micah had prophesied that "Zion shall be plowed like a field". Did Hezekiah put Micah to death? No. Hezekiah repented and sought forgiveness. The result was that the Lord turned away his anger. The wisdom of these elders must have sealed the verdict. Jeremiah could go free.

But another prophet did not escape. Urijah the son of Shemaiah of Kirjath-jearim was moved to reiterate the words of Jeremiah: "When Jehoiakim the king, with all his mighty men, and all the princes, heard his words, the king sought to put him to death: but when Urijah heard it, he was afraid, and fled, and went into Egypt: and Jehoiakim the king sent men into Egypt ... and they fetched forth Urijah out of Egypt, and brought him unto Jehoiakim the king; who slew him with the sword, and cast his dead body into the graves of the common people" (verses 21-23). The detailed account of this incident emphasises just how far Jehoiakim was prepared to go to silence the witness of the Word of God. Jeremiah had been saved because there was a groundswell of support from the nobility and the people themselves. And Jeremiah also had friends in high places who looked after his well-being; notably, Ahikam the son of Shaphan (verse 24). But Jehoiakim could not tolerate the development of any movement in support of Jeremiah and so he silenced Urijah: "This hath been thy manner from thy youth, that thou obeyedst not my voice."

The Battle of Carchemish

The fourth year of Jehoiakim's reign was a significant time because it was also the first year of the reign of Nebuchadnezzar. It was the year that the military contest for Palestine between the rising power of Babylon, and the ageing power of Egypt came to a decisive conclusion. In that year, 605 BC, in early summer, a Babylonian army under the leadership of Nebuchadnezzar surprised the Egyptians at Carchemish and routed them (Jeremiah 46:2). As he was pursuing the fleeing remnant of the Egyptian army, Nebuchadnezzar heard of the death of his father Nabopolassar. Nebuchadnezzar rushed back to Babylon to secure the throne, but his army took over the vassal states of Palestine, including Judah, taking captives back with them to Babylon. Amongst these captives were Daniel, Hananiah, Mishael and Azariah. The following year Nebuchadnezzar returned formally to make Jehoiakim his servant (2 Kings 24:1). Jehoiakim was living in momentous times but he was oblivious to their prophetic significance. The prophecy of Jeremiah 25, given in Jehoiakim's fourth year, contains the promise of the seventy years of captivity in Babylon. How would Jehoiakim respond?

Jeremiah 36 also begins in the fourth year of Jehoiakim's reign. Jeremiah is told to write in a book all the prophecies that he has been given. This he did using Baruch as the scribe. Jehoiakim at this time must have put Jeremiah under house arrest because Jeremiah said to Baruch, "I am shut up; I cannot go into the house of the LORD: therefore go thou, and read in the roll" (verses 5,6). Baruch was then sent to read the book out loud in the temple. The longsuffering of God was giving the nation yet one more opportunity to repent (verse 7). Baruch read the prophecy in the hearing of all the people in the temple on a special "fasting day" in the fifth year and the ninth month of Jehoiakim's reign. Clearly, by this time Jehoiakim could do with all the help he could get!

News of Baruch's preaching effort reached the privy council and Baruch was summoned to bring the book and read it to the princes who were gathered in the palace. These rulers again showed a surprisingly sympathetic attitude to Baruch and Jeremiah. On hearing the prophecies the princes were very concerned for their safety and warned Baruch that he and Jeremiah should hide from the wrath of the king. But the book itself was "laid up" in the chamber of Elishama the scribe (verse 20). The respect shown by the princes to that Word of God is very interesting. It was still only six years since the death of Josiah and their reverence for the book of Jeremiah must be traced back to Josiah's influence. And yet Josiah's son was to demonstrate that he had absolutely no regard for the book.

When Jehoiakim heard what had transpired he sent for the scroll and Jehudi read it to him as he sat by the fire. "And it came to pass, that when Jehudi had read three or four leaves, he cut it with the penknife, and cast it into the fire that was on the hearth, until all the roll was consumed in the fire" (verse 23). The complete disdain with which Jehoiakim held the Word of God was blatantly demonstrated in the picture of the king, casually slicing off the sections of the book of the prophecy of Jeremiah as they were being read to him, and watching the flames lick up the shreds of Baruch's handwriting as he threw them on the fire. The record draws attention to this contemptuous dismissal of Jeremiah's prophecy in a tone of disbelief: "Yet they were not afraid, nor rent their garments, neither the king, nor any of his servants that heard all these words" (verse 24). Despite the efforts of Elnathan and Delaiah and Gemariah to prevent the king burning the roll, "he would not hear them": "This hath been thy manner from thy youth, that thou obeyedst not my voice."

This happened in the fifth year of his reign, which was also the second year of Nebuchadnezzar's reign. What a tremendous irony there is here. The second year of Nebuchadnezzar was the year in which God revealed to him in a dream the future of the kingdom of men recorded in Daniel 2, and when "Nebuchadnezzar fell upon his face" before Daniel because of the awe in which he held the prophet of the living God. And yet the Word of God which Josiah had so cherished was discarded as refuse by his son. But the Word of God cannot be destroyed. The Lord commanded Jeremiah to write out the prophecies again and to tell Jehoiakim that he was to be killed at the hands of the King of Babylon, who himself had trembled at the Word of God.

A Postscript for Baruch

Jeremiah 45 is a short letter to Baruch after he had completed the task of writing out the prophecies of Jeremiah for the first time. Baruch's thoughts at that time were revealed by the Lord: "Thou didst say, Woe is me now! for the LORD hath added grief to my sorrow; I fainted in my sighing, and I find no rest" (verse 3). Was it the content of the prophecies which so disturbed him, the destruction of Jerusalem and the end of the kingdom? Was it the prospect of having to go into the temple and read out such bad news to the people? After all, no one likes being the bearer of evil tidings, even if they have no responsibility for the evil events. But there was more to Baruch's distress. He was a man who had ambitions: not necessarily worldly ambitions, but plans which the fulfilment of Jeremiah's prophecies would thwart. And the Lord answers these thoughts with the words: "Thus shalt thou say unto him, The LORD saith thus; Behold, that which I have built will I break down, and that which I have planted I will pluck up, even this whole land. And seekest thou great things for thyself? seek them not: for, behold, I will bring evil upon all flesh, saith the LORD: but thy life will I give unto thee for a prey in all places whither thou goest" (verses 4,5).

Baruch is here reminded that the land and the kingdom in which he planned a career was God's land and God's kingdom and He would do with it as He pleased. Here is a warning for us today. We may plan a career, plot out a course in life, and forget that we are not our own; we are bought with a price and he who bought us desires that we "seek first the kingdom of God and his righteousness". If in the day of the Lord's return we are given what Baruch was promised – his life for a prey – we shall surely consider that our most worthy ambition has been fulfilled.

The Judgement of Jehoiakim

Jehoiakim had been placed on the throne originally by Pharaoh-Necho, and Judah was paying tribute to Egypt. But in the fourth year of his reign control of Palestine was surrendered to Babylon. In such circumstances one might imagine that Jehoiakim would see the need to turn to the Lord, as Jeremiah so many times tries to tell him: but not this renegade son of Josiah. The prophecy of Ezekiel 19 appears to be a commentary on the response of Jehoiakim to the political crisis he faced. Jehoiakim's predecessor Jehoahaz is the subject of verse 4: "The nations also heard of him; he was taken in their pit, and they brought him with chains unto the land of Egypt." Attention then passes to Jehoiakim:

"Now when she (the nation) saw that she had waited, and her hope was lost, then she took another of her whelps, and made him a young lion. And he ... learned to catch the prey, and devoured men. And he knew their desolate palaces, and he laid waste their cities ... Then the nations set against him on every side from the provinces, and spread their net over him: he was taken in their pit. And they put him in ward in chains, and brought him to the king of Babylon." (verses 5-9)

This account suggests that Jehoiakim had attacked his neighbouring states: he became "a young lion", and "learned to catch the prey". But eventually these states combined to destroy the kingdom of Judah: "And the LORD sent against him bands of the Chaldees, and bands of the

131

Syrians, and bands of the Moabites, and bands of the children of Ammon, and sent them against Judah to destroy it, according to the word of the LORD, which he spake by his servants the prophets" (2 Kings 24:2). Ezekiel 19 indicates that these adversaries of Jehoiakim captured him and took him bound in chains to Nebuchadnezzar. Exactly when this happened is not absolutely clear but we have to put these events together with those described in 2 Chronicles 36 and Jeremiah 36.

The sequence of events according to F. F. Bruce was as follows:

"In 601 BC Nebuchadrezzar led an army to the Egyptian frontier to give battle to Necho, but this time he suffered severe losses, from which he took eighteen months to recover. Many of his new vassals immediately withheld tribute from him, including Jehoiakim [as referred to in 2 Kings 24:1]. But when Nebuchadrezzar had repaired the losses in his manpower and equipment, he marched west again, and put down the rebels one by one. He dealt first with Arab tribes east and south of Judah, and meanwhile incited Jehoiakim's neighbours to attack him."*

These enemies must have caught Jehoiakim and brought him in chains to Nebuchadnezzar who then took custody of the king of Judah. 2 Chronicles 36 says, "Against him came up Nebuchadnezzar king of Babylon, and bound him in fetters, to carry him to Babylon" (verse 5).

That must have been his intention, but before the journey to Babylon could be undertaken Jehoiakim died. Jeremiah had prophesied of this day: "Therefore thus saith the LORD of Jehoiakim king of Judah; He shall have none to sit upon the throne of David: and his dead body shall be cast out in the day to the heat, and in the night to the frost" (Jeremiah 36:30). Denied the pleasure of parading his captive king through the streets of Babylon, Nebuchadnezzar appears to have exhibited the body of the prematurely dead Jehoiakim, perhaps before the walls of Jerusalem, as he was laying siege to it. And there was to

---

* *Israel and the Nations*, page 88 (Second Impression, 1965; published by The Paternoster Press).

be no decent burial for Jehoiakim: "Therefore thus saith the LORD concerning Jehoiakim the son of Josiah king of Judah; They shall not lament for him, saying, Ah my brother! or, Ah sister! they shall not lament for him, saying, Ah lord! or, Ah his glory! He shall be buried with the burial of an ass, drawn and cast forth beyond the gates of Jerusalem" (22:18,19).

This reference to mourning is interesting because in part it is a quotation from 1 Kings 13, the prophecy of the coming of Josiah to destroy the apostate religion at Bethel. In that chapter, as we have seen, the man of God who had delivered the prophecy against Bethel was killed himself because he failed to follow the will of God. He had been sidetracked from his mission by the old prophet of Bethel and in consequence a lion in the way had slain him. The old prophet buried the man of God in his own grave, "and they mourned over him, saying, Alas, my brother!" (verse 30). So even a man who had strayed from the right way had been mourned over. But not Jehoiakim. There was no dignity in the death of a man who not only disobeyed the Word of God but despised it. And there is exhortation in this for us. If we should ever despise the Word of God and turn away from the Truth, all that will remain for us is "a certain fearful looking for of judgment and fiery indignation, which shall devour the adversaries" (Hebrews 10:27).

Here then was the grim end to a man who, despite his good upbringing, sought the ways which are abomination to God (2 Chronicles 36:8). Jehoiakim was dishonest and exploited the poor and needy (Jeremiah 22:13); he was materialistic, covetous and proud (22:14,17); he surrounded himself with worldly friends (26:21), hated the true prophets of God (26:12-23) and was deaf to wise counsel (36:25). What a terrible character. And this was Josiah's eldest son! May his life be a warning to each one of us to consider very carefully how we are responding to the voice of the living God.

16

JEHOIACHIN – A DESPISED BROKEN IDOL?

FOLLOWING the ignominious death of Jehoiakim, the kingdom passed to his son Jehoiachin who was eighteen years old when he began to reign.* He reigned just three months like his uncle Jehoahaz, and like his uncle nothing good can be said of him: "He did that which was evil in the sight of the LORD" (2 Chronicles 36:9). The 2 Kings record adds, "according to all that his father had done" (2 Kings 24:9).

Jehoiachin would have been just old enough to have definite memories of Josiah; he was seven when his grandfather died. He should have had an understanding of how precious the Word of God was to Josiah, and he should have realised in what high regard the prophets of Yahweh were esteemed at that time. Furthermore, he probably was a junior member of the royal youth group which numbered amongst its older members Daniel, Hananiah, Mishael and Azariah before they, as "the king's seed", were taken into Babylon when Jehoiachin was 10 years old. But such positive early memories can be easily overwritten by the teenage influences to which he must have yielded.

---

* The 2 Chronicles 36:9 record says that Jehoiachin was 8 years old when he began to reign, apparently contradicting the 2 Kings record. Is this a copyist's error or is there another explanation? Martin Anstey offered this explanation: "Both statements are equally true, but the two writers who make them reckon the years from a different starting point ... the same year was also the 8th year of Nebuchadnezzar, and it is this fact which was in the mind of the writer of 2 Chronicles 36:9, when he said, "Jehoiachin was" a son of 8 years "when he began to reign". The expression "son of" is used with a great deal of latitude ... Here the words are used to express the number of years between the accession of Jehoiachin and the 1st year of the new era of the reign of Nebuchadnezzar"—*The Romance of Bible Chronology*, Vol. 1, 1913, page 223.

Unworthy of the Name!

Jehoiachin appears to have been known also by the name of Jeconiah (see 1 Chronicles 3:16), but he is counted unworthy to bear the name of God – "Yah" – and is known as Coniah to the prophet Jeremiah:

"As I live, saith the LORD, though Coniah the son of Jehoiakim king of Judah were the signet upon my right hand, yet would I pluck thee thence; and I will give thee into the hand of them that seek thy life, and into the hand of them whose face thou fearest, even into the hand of Nebuchadrezzar king of Babylon, and into the hand of the Chaldeans. And I will cast thee out, and thy mother that bare thee, into another country, where ye were not born; and there shall ye die. But to the land whereunto they desire to return, thither shall they not return." (Jeremiah 22:24-27)

The "signet" on the right hand is a reference to the signet ring which held the official seal of the king and thereby the authority to confirm laws and statutes. It would therefore represent the rulership of the kingdom (compare Genesis 41:42). But the prophecy says "though" Coniah was the signet, suggesting the sense of 'even if' he were the signet. This raises the question of whether Jehoiachin was indeed the rightful king. Certainly by genealogy he appears to have been, but he was not going to be in the line of David's seed which would lead directly to Christ. Is the prophecy saying here that even if he was to be in direct line to Messiah (rather than to Joseph, Mary's husband) yet still God would cast him out of the kingdom? How tragic that by the age of eighteen the young man's fate was already sealed.

Jehoiachin was to be cast out of the kingdom with his mother. She was Nehushta the daughter of Elnathan. Her name means 'brazen', which may have been an appropriate description of her character. The fact that she was to share the judgement which would come on the king suggests that she in large measure shared the responsibility for the way her son had grown up. How important is a mother's influence over her children! In the record of Jeremiah 22 stress is placed upon their relation

135

to the land of Judah. They were told that they were to go into "another country, where ye were not born".

Furthermore, the land of Judah was a land to which they would "desire to return" but would not. Then Jeremiah makes an appeal as it were to that land: "O earth, earth, earth, hear the word of the LORD" (verse 29). It seems that the land had a very special place in their affections and they dreaded the prospect of being taken from it. Jehoiachin's uncle Jehoahaz had been exiled to Egypt and was not coming back; his father Jehoiakim had been sentenced to go to Babylon but died before that could happen. And now there was the real threat that Nebuchadnezzar would return and do the same to Jehoiachin. Jeremiah confirms that the king's worst fears were indeed going to come true: "And I will give thee into the hand of them that seek thy life, and into the hand of them whose face thou fearest" (verse 25).

The description of Jehoiachin's character, and the judgements which were to come upon him as recounted by Jeremiah, draw a number of parallels between the king and the nation of Israel through the centuries. For example, in the prophecy of Hosea 8:8 the nation is described in the same terms that Jeremiah uses of Jehoiachin. Hosea says, "Israel is swallowed up: now shall they be among the Gentiles as a vessel wherein is no pleasure". Jeremiah quotes these words when he asks, "Is this man Coniah a despised broken idol? is he a vessel wherein is no pleasure? wherefore are they cast out, he and his seed, and are cast into a land which they know not?" (22:28). Jehoiachin, as the last proper king to sit on the throne of David, symbolises the frame of mind of the people. Consider Israel in the first century AD, so deeply attached to the land, but unwilling to live in a way which would secure their inheritance of it. And just as Jehoiachin's worst fears were to come upon him, so for the nation then, "They shall fall by the edge of the sword, and shall be led away captive into all nations: and Jerusalem shall be trodden down of the Gentiles ..." (Luke 21:24).

"Write this man childless!"

The final part of Jeremiah's pronouncement upon Jehoiachin was devastating: "Thus saith the LORD, Write

136

ye this man childless, a man that shall not prosper in his days: for no man of his seed shall prosper, sitting upon the throne of David, and ruling any more in Judah" (22:30). But what does it mean? This has been a problem passage over the years. But note that it does not say that Jehoiachin would not have any children. Scripture in other places says that he did. It says, "Write ye this man childless". The idea of writing would have to do with an official line of descent, a pedigree which gave entitlement to the throne. Jehoiachin was not to have that privilege. Once Jehoiachin and then his uncle Zedekiah were taken away, the throne of David would be vacated until the Lord Jesus Christ would return from heaven to rule the earth in righteousness – "Remove the diadem, and take off the crown ... I will overturn, overturn, overturn, it: and it shall be no more, until he come whose right it is; and I will give it him" (Ezekiel 21:26,27). And so it was the case that no descendant of Jehoiachin sat upon the throne of David ruling any more in Judah. Jehoiachin did have a grandson, Zerubbabel, who was the leader of the remnant of Judah which returned to build the temple after the seventy year captivity, but he was not king and did not sit upon the throne of David. Zerubbabel was, however, a faithful servant of his God and because of that he was promised something which marvellously cancelled out every negative thing which was associated with his grandfather. Through the prophet Haggai, Zerubbabel was told of the time when the kingdom which had been overturned by Babylon would be restored, and when the nations which trampled Jerusalem under foot would themselves be overturned: "And I will overthrow the throne of kingdoms, and I will destroy the strength of the kingdoms of the heathen; and I will overthrow the chariots, and those that ride in them ... In that day, saith the LORD of hosts, will I take thee, O Zerubbabel, my servant, the son of Shealtiel, saith the LORD, and will make thee as a signet: for I have chosen thee" (2:23).

Jehoiachin was likened to a signet which was no longer of any value, a seal which no longer carried any weight, but Zerubbabel will, in the Kingdom of God be counted worthy to carry responsibility under the direction of

Christ. He will be a "king" to rule with Christ on David's throne. And this is the promise offered to all those who turn away from the fashions of this world and seek first the Kingdom of God and His righteousness. Jehoiachin succumbed to the influences of his ungodly family and a society besotted with the worship of pleasure, but the Lord Jesus Christ promises, "To him that overcometh will I grant to sit with me in my throne, even as I also overcame, and am set down with my Father in his throne" (Revelation 3:21). God is even now calling out of the Gentiles a "people for his name" and promises to "build again the tabernacle of David, which is fallen down" (Acts 15:14-16). If we want to have that name written upon our foreheads (Revelation 14:1), as a seal that we belong to Christ, then we must be sure in our daily lives to honour the One who has called us, "that the name of God and his doctrine be not blasphemed" (1 Timothy 6:1).

"A vessel wherein is no pleasure"

So why was Jehoiachin judged so harshly? The answer is given by Jeremiah. Jehoiachin was "a despised broken idol", a "vessel wherein is no pleasure". He was a broken pot which was not fit to be used in the house, unable to hold its measure, tipping up and spilling its contents – a man who did not realise his potential. The vessel was to be cast out and smashed. The picture is familiar to us from Jeremiah's prophecies, and may have been familiar to Jehoiachin. In chapter 18, Jeremiah was instructed to go to the potter's house and watch the potter form a vessel from the clay. The first attempt was faulty and so the potter remoulded the clay and started again. Could not God do the same to Israel? (verse 6).

This was in fact a message of hope. If they turned from their evil ways and yielded themselves to God He would reform them. Indeed this had been the appeal which God had made to the northern kingdom just a few years before they were taken away by the Assyrians. Through the offices of King Hezekiah, Israel were asked to "turn again" and "yield" beneath the hand of God (2 Chronicles 30:6-8). But a "stiffnecked" people cannot yield. They hardened themselves in the form which the potter did not want. They said, "We will everyone do the imagination of his evil heart" (Jeremiah 18:12). The "evil heart" of unbelief had led to the demise of Israel in the wilderness (Hebrews 3:12), and now Jeremiah is shown what was to happen to them. A nation which had stiffened itself against the influence of the Word of God through the mouth of the prophets was like clay which had been baked in the oven, unable to be remodelled. If it was so out of shape that it could not be of use, it would be cast away and smashed. In chapter 19 of his prophecy Jeremiah is told to enact this picture. He is told to take "a potter's earthen bottle" and go with the elders to the valley of the son of Hinnom. There he was to pronounce the terrible events of the siege of Jerusalem, and then break the bottle and say to the witnesses, "Thus saith the LORD of hosts; Even so will I break this people and this city, as one breaketh a potter's vessel, that cannot be made whole again: and they shall bury them in Tophet, till there be no place to bury" (19:11). The harder and more brittle the clay, the greater number of pieces it would shatter into!

The lesson of the potter applies equally well to us as to Jehoiachin. We must yield ourselves to the hand of God, acknowledging Him in all our ways, being "exercised" by the chastening circumstances of life (Hebrews 12:11), rather than being hardened and embittered (verse 15). The difficulties which come our way are intended by the Father to cause us to turn to Him with all our hearts, and He will not let us down. And in the process of being exercised we shall be moulded into vessels which He can use in His Kingdom. We all desire to be "vessels unto honour, sanctified, and meet for the master's use, and prepared unto every good work" (2 Timothy 2:21). Therefore we have to "flee also youthful lusts: but follow righteousness, faith, charity, peace, with them that call on the Lord out of a pure heart" (verse 22). Did Paul have Jehoiachin in mind by way of contrast when he penned these words to Timothy?

A Vessel of Mercy?

We wonder whether Jehoiachin did think on such things after Jeremiah had likened him to a "vessel wherein is no pleasure". Would he necessarily be a "vessel of wrath fitted to destruction"? Or might he become a "vessel of mercy ... prepared unto glory"? Certainly there is no mention in the Scriptures of any conversion of Jehoiachin, but his life story does reveal the providential hand of God watching over him. Though Jehoiachin was counted as a worthless vessel as far as the kingdom of Judah was concerned, no longer able to pass the throne of David to his descendants, he was to be spared death in order that the family tree could continue down to Joseph, and so give Jesus, by virtue of that line, the right to the throne of David in the eyes of the nation. Jehoiachin is mentioned in the genealogy of the Lord in Matthew 1. This is not the physical line of descent of Christ; it ends with Joseph, the Lord's stepfather. But as Joseph's official son the line proved that Jesus was the rightful heir to the throne of David. (And if that could be proved from the official records which we are told were kept in the temple during those times, is it possible that this genealogy was one reason why the Jews were envious of him and sought to kill him? "This is the heir; come, let us kill him, and let us seize on his inheritance" (Matthew 21:38).

The way in which Jehoiachin was saved to father the royal line (though not to provide a king to sit on David's throne) is remarkable. The Babylonians did return and took Jehoiachin captive, together with "the goodly vessels of the house of the LORD" (2 Chronicles 36:10). The record says: "At that time the servants of Nebuchadnezzar king of Babylon came up against Jerusalem, and the city was besieged. And Nebuchadnezzar king of Babylon came against the city, and his servants did besiege it. And Jehoiachin the king of Judah went out to the king of Babylon, he, and his mother, and his servants, and his princes, and his officers" (2 Kings 24:10-12). The twofold reference to the siege in these verses draws attention to the coming of Nebuchadnezzar personally to join his troops and the effect that had upon Jehoiachin. At the appearance of Nebuchadnezzar Jehoiachin immediately submitted to the man he so greatly feared.

Surprisingly perhaps Jehoiachin found mercy at the hand of Nebuchadnezzar. Was this the influence of Daniel who by this time was ruler of Babylon? And was it Daniel who ensured that the king was well looked after in

Babylon, though a prisoner and exile? Clay tablets have been found in the ruins of ancient Babylon which make reference to Jehoiachin, even giving him his official title as "King of the land of Judah". The tablets are dated the thirteenth year of the reign of the king Nebuchadnezzar, 592 BC, five or six years after he was taken captive. They record food rations which were allocated to Jehoiachin and his company. Later on –

"It came to pass in the seven and thirtieth year of the captivity of Jehoiachin king of Judah, in the twelfth month, on the seven and twentieth day of the month, that Evil-merodach king of Babylon in the year that he began to reign did lift up the head of Jehoiachin king of Judah out of prison; and he spake kindly to him, and set his throne above the throne of the kings that were with him in Babylon; and changed his prison garments: and he did eat bread continually before him all the days of his life. And his allowance was a continual allowance given him of the king, a daily rate for every day, all the days of his life." (2 Kings 25:27-30)
(see also Jeremiah 52:31-34)

The detail given here of such apparently mundane matters as food rations needs to be explained, as does the fact that an almost identical account is to be found as the last words of the book of the prophet Jeremiah. There is a marvellous tie-up with the archaeological discoveries, but why are we told these things? At the simplest level the events proved that God was indeed in control of His people, and had a purpose with them even when they were suffering the punishment of their disobedience. The elevation of Jehoiachin may have signalled the relaxation of restraint upon the Jews, assisting in the spiritual development of the remnant who were to eschew the idols of their fathers and return to rebuild Jerusalem in sincerity and truth. And if Jehoiachin in his punishment was a type of the nation of Israel, a hardened pot unfit for use, then the preservation of his life in Babylon would represent the unique survival of the Jews, though dispersed amongst the Gentiles, until the time was right to be regathered to their land. The captivity of Jehoiachin does seem to be used in this way in the prophecy of

Ezekiel, providing the reference point for dates throughout the book.

With Jehoiachin going into captivity were the skilled craftsmen, "carpenters and smiths", some of whom would have worked with Josiah in the repairing of the house of God. How tragic for them in particular to see "all the treasures of the house of the LORD, and the treasures of the king's house" (2 Kings 24:13) and the vessels which Solomon had made for the temple, cut in pieces and taken as booty. What profit had they in all their labour? But these were the "good figs" mentioned by Jeremiah in chapter 24 of his prophecy. They were taken away "for their good", and Jehoiachin shared in the blessing which went with them. Their captivity was accompanied by the hope of return. Not for Jehoiachin, as falsely promised by Hananiah the son of Azur (Jeremiah 28:4), but for those who would patiently wait for the hand of God to work out His revealed will. To this end Jeremiah sent them a letter recorded in chapter 29 of his prophecy. It told them to build houses, have families, seek the peace of the place where they were taken, refuse the false visions of those who prophesied lies, and wait upon the Lord until the seventy years were passed. How very much like the circumstances of the saints waiting for the return of the Lord Jesus Christ, although we do not know how many years – or months, or weeks – that will be. And during this period of waiting, we are to pray to our Heavenly Father that He will "give us this day our daily bread" (as he gave it to Jehoiachin), and deliver us from evil, until His kingdom comes.

17

ZEDEKIAH THE TWILIGHT PRINCE

ONCE Jehoiachin was taken into captivity in Babylon, Nebuchadnezzar put Mattaniah on the throne of Judah and changed his name to Zedekiah. Zedekiah was Josiah's third son and therefore Jehoiachin's uncle. He was about 13 years younger than his brother Jehoahaz and 15 years younger than Jehoiakim: a big enough gap, one might think, to avoid the worst influences of those wayward young men. However, the Scriptures state that when Zedekiah came to the throne, "he did that which was evil in the sight of the LORD, according to all that Jehoiakim had done" (2 Kings 24:19). Does this indicate that Zedekiah saw his older brother as a rôle model to follow? Certainly it is the case today that young people in our own youth groups and ecclesias will, whether they are aware of it or not, leave a powerful impression on the minds of younger ones who will look up to them and tend to follow their examples, for good or ill.

Zedekiah was born after the discovery of the Word of God, and for the first ten years or so of his life he would have had the sweet influence of his father to inspire him. Furthermore, as he passed through the teenage years he would have seen the way in which his brothers so ignobly met their end, and how the Word of the true prophets of Yahweh had been vindicated. It is therefore all the more remarkable that Zedekiah showed such disdain for the Word of God. In particular, it is his treatment of Jeremiah's prophecies for which he is held most responsible. The record is at pains to point out the rôle which Jeremiah had in the reign of Zedekiah and subsequent events: "Zedekiah was one and twenty years old when he began to reign, and reigned eleven years in Jerusalem. And he did that which was evil in the sight of the LORD his God, and humbled not himself before

Jeremiah the prophet speaking from the mouth of the LORD" (2 Chronicles 36:12). All that happened to Jerusalem and the house of God as a result of the final Babylonian invasion happened "to fulfil the word of the LORD by the mouth of Jeremiah" (verse 21), and the eventual restoration to the land seventy years later is described in similar terms: "Now in the first year of Cyrus king of Persia, that the word of the LORD spoken by the mouth of Jeremiah might be accomplished ..." (verse 22). Clearly, when we seek to understand this section of the history of God's people we shall need to look closely at the interaction between Jeremiah and Zedekiah.

Not a Man of his Word

The Chronicles record of the reign of Zedekiah draws attention to one particular aspect of his behaviour: "He also rebelled against king Nebuchadnezzar, who had made him swear by God: but he stiffened his neck, and hardened his heart from turning unto the LORD God of Israel" (2 Chronicles 36:13). The prophet Ezekiel, from his home in the captivity of Babylon, is also brought to denounce this treacherous act of Zedekiah, and the account gives us more of an insight into what lay behind the rebellion. Ezekiel says:

"But he rebelled against him in sending his ambassadors into Egypt, that they might give him horses and much people. Shall he prosper? shall he escape that doeth such things? or shall he break the covenant, and be delivered? As I live, saith the Lord GOD, surely in the place where the king dwelleth that made him king, whose oath he despised, and whose covenant he brake, even with him in the midst of Babylon he shall die."   (Ezekiel 17:15,16)

The same chapter of Ezekiel goes on to emphasise that the oath of allegiance to Nebuchadnezzar was a covenant before God: "Therefore thus saith the Lord GOD; As I live, surely mine oath that he hath despised, and my covenant that he hath broken, even it will I recompense upon his own head" (verse 19). Was this because the peace agreement arranged by Nebuchadnezzar had been set up through Daniel's influence in Babylon, a merciful provision of the God of Israel to prevent the usual

144

brutality which would be expected in ancient conflicts? It is a salutary thought that God views the failure to honour a vow so seriously. The vows we make at baptism and in marriage are lifelong vows and they must surely be kept as covenants with God.

Another example which shows the difficulty Zedekiah had in keeping his promises is in Jeremiah 34. The same chapter describes how Zedekiah had made an attempt to turn back to God, perhaps under the close influence of Jeremiah during the first Babylonian siege. He had made a covenant to honour the year of release and set the slaves free. The people and princes followed the king's lead, for a while at least; "but afterward they turned", when it seems the Babylonians temporarily withdrew due to the advancing Egyptian army (see verse 22), and the rulers took their former servants back into slavery (verse 11). The denunciation of the Lord was severe. They had done right in making a covenant before the Lord in the house "which is called by my name" (verse 15), but they had turned and polluted God's name. As a consequence the sword, pestilence and famine would wreak vengeance upon them (verse 17), and Zedekiah would go into captivity (verse 21). Zedekiah was a man with no depth of soil for the Word to take root, a vacillating king who did not set an example of constancy for the people to follow. What a contrast with his single-minded and determined father! The Psalmist asked: "LORD, who shall abide in thy tabernacle? who shall dwell in thy holy hill?" Part of the answer was, "He that sweareth to his own hurt, and changeth not" (15:1,4).

Zedekiah Caught in a Net

As a result of Zedekiah's rebellion, "It came to pass in the ninth year of his reign, in the tenth month, in the tenth day of the month, that Nebuchadnezzar king of Babylon came, and all his host, against Jerusalem, and pitched against it; and they built forts against it round about. And the city was besieged unto the eleventh year of the king Zedekiah. And on the ninth day of the fourth month the famine prevailed in the city, and there was no bread for the people of the land" (2 Kings 25:1-3). It was a tragic period for the inhabitants of the city. In his Lamentations

145

Jeremiah describes the scene in terrible detail: "Mine eyes do fail with tears, my bowels are troubled, my liver is poured upon the earth, for the destruction of the daughter of my people; because the children and the sucklings swoon in the streets of the city. They say to their mothers, Where is corn and wine?" (2:11,12); "The hands of the pitiful women have sodden their own children: they were their meat in the destruction of the daughter of my people" (4:10).

This horrible scene was the result of God's judgements upon a city wholly given over to vice, but it could have been prevented by Zedekiah had he the courage to submit to the counsel of Jeremiah. Jeremiah had said to him, "Bring your necks under the yoke of the king of Babylon, and serve him and his people, and live. Why will ye die, thou and thy people, by the sword, by the famine, and by the pestilence?" (Jeremiah 27:12,13). But the stiff neck of Zedekiah could not bend sufficiently to come under that yoke.

At the end of the siege, when the defences collapsed, Zedekiah fled from the city "by night by the way of the gate between the two walls, which is by the king's garden" (2 Kings 25:4). Deserting the people he had led into an unnecessary disaster of the most terrible sort, the cowardly king made use of his pre-planned escape route. He got as far as the plains of Jericho with some at least of his soldiers, but the Babylonians caught up with them. He was taken before Nebuchadnezzar in Riblah and there was called to account (verse 6).

The prophet Ezekiel had earlier predicted the events which were to follow. He had to enact the captivity of the king by moving his belongings from his home into another house, and then at twilight break through the wall of the house and carry out his belongings upon his shoulders, "as they that go forth into captivity" (Ezekiel 12:4). Ezekiel had to cover his face so that he could not see the ground. He goes on to say: "I did so as I was commanded: I brought forth my stuff by day, as stuff for captivity, and in the even I digged through the wall with mine hand; I brought it forth in the twilight, and I bare it upon my shoulder in their sight" (verse 7). The explanation for this extraordinary parable was specifically to do with Zedekiah: "The prince that is among them shall bear upon his shoulder in the twilight, and shall go forth: they shall dig through the wall to carry out thereby: he shall cover his face, that he see not the ground with his eyes" (verse 12). The prophecy goes on to tell how the humiliated king would be taken into Babylon itself: "My net also will I spread upon him, and he shall be taken in my snare: and I will bring him to Babylon to the land of the Chaldeans; yet shall he not see it, though he shall die there" (verse 13).

This latter detail – "yet shall he not see it" – was ominous indeed. When Zedekiah was brought before Nebuchadnezzar, "they slew the sons of Zedekiah before his eyes, and put out the eyes of Zedekiah, and bound him with fetters of brass, and carried him to Babylon" (2 Kings 25:7). What thoughts would Daniel have had as he saw the last king of Judah taken so forlornly through the streets of the great city, a man who during his reign was blind to the Word of God, now sightless and with his last visual memory the sight of his sons being slain! In Babylon Zedekiah was put in prison until the day of his death (Jeremiah 52:11). The words of Ezekiel would ring in his ears and in the ears of all those who pondered the prophecy of the dreadful days of 587 BC: "And thou, profane wicked prince of Israel, whose day is come, when iniquity shall have an end, Thus saith the Lord GOD; Remove the diadem, and take off the crown: this shall not be the same: exalt him that is low, and abase him that is high. I will overturn, overturn, overturn, it: and it shall be no more, until he come whose right it is; and I will give it him" (Ezekiel 21:25-27).

A Hearer but not a Doer of the Word

The tragedy of the life of Zedekiah is made the more poignant because there is something about Zedekiah that we can warm to, although at the end of his life he is dismissed by the Lord as that wicked and profane prince whose time was come. The fact that Yahweh is called "his God" in 2 Chronicles 36:12 is perhaps some indication that he had a belief in the One True God, although not a sufficient faith to lead a life which would honour the Lord.

There was a spark in Zedekiah; he did have some interest in the Word of God, but it was never sufficient to catch light. The prophecy of Ezekiel 12 in which he is portrayed in the "twilight" sums up his character. In the things of God light and darkness are opposites – they cannot co-exist. A man is either light or he is darkness before the Lord: "What communion hath light with darkness?" (2 Corinthians 6:14); "For ye were sometimes darkness, but now are ye light in the Lord: walk as children of light" (Ephesians 5:8). The shadowy places of compromise, where we may seek to hide, neither fully committed to the Lord nor fully immersed in the world, is no place for the disciple of Christ. But this was the land Zedekiah inhabited.

Zedekiah appears to have had an interest in, and respect for, the prophecies of Jeremiah, though perhaps he was seeking a sentimental comfort he associated with his childhood and his father Josiah. In Jeremiah 21 we read a prophecy which is introduced with the words:

> "The word which came unto Jeremiah from the LORD, when king Zedekiah sent unto him Pashur the son of Melchiah, and Zephaniah the son of Maaseiah the priest, saying, Enquire, I pray thee, of the LORD for us; for Nebuchadnezzar king of Babylon maketh war against us; if so be that the LORD will deal with us according to all his wondrous works, that he may go up from us." (verses 1,2)

Was Zedekiah harking back to the teaching of his father Josiah now that he was in desperate trouble and the "prophets" which he had surrounded himself with could not help? The answer from the Lord contained none of the comforts of childhood which he may have been looking for: "I myself will fight against you with an outstretched hand and with a strong arm, even in anger, and in fury, and in great wrath" (verse 5); "He shall not spare them, neither have pity, nor have mercy" (verse 7). And why was this severe punishment to come upon the king? Because he did not execute judgement in the morning or "deliver him that is spoiled out of the hand of the oppressor" (verse 12). The twilight king was not there "in the morning" when he was needed!

It is a curious thing that men and women can derive a sentimental enjoyment from exhortation, even though they have no intention of changing their ways to follow the Word of God. Of the prophet Ezekiel the Scriptures say:

"They come unto thee as the people cometh, and they sit before thee as my people, and they hear thy words, but they will not do them: for with their mouth they shew much love, but their heart goeth after their covetousness. And, lo, thou art unto them as a very lovely song of one that hath a pleasant voice, and can play well on an instrument: for they hear thy words, but they do them not."   (Ezekiel 33:31,32)

A Secret Seeker after God

The prophecies of Jeremiah were judged to be subversive by the ruling princes who placed him under house arrest. He was "shut up in the court of the prison, which was in the king of Judah's house" (Jeremiah 32:2); interestingly, close enough to the king for private consultation, but far enough away from the people not to demoralise them. And there appears to have been close and frequent contact between Jeremiah and the king. Zedekiah must have heard not only the gloomy prophecies of defeat at the hands of the Babylonians but also the glorious prophecies of the Kingdom of God on earth. In all probability he witnessed the transaction of Jeremiah 32 when Jeremiah bought a field in the land of Anathoth from his cousin Hanameel. The command to buy the field was a token of the certainty of Israel's restoration when God would "gather them out of all countries" (verse 37), when they would be His people and He would be their God (verse 38), and when fields would be bought again in the land (verse 43). Zedekiah would have heard the promise of Jeremiah 33 which spoke of the time when Jerusalem would be filled with the praises of the Lord and a righteous Branch would sit upon David's throne (verse 15). Certainly, Zedekiah heard the gospel being preached in the courtyard of his own house. For this reason Zedekiah's responsibility before God was great.

In Jeremiah 37 we get an insight into the moral weakness of the king. There had been a temporary respite from the siege. Pharaoh had come out of Egypt and the

Babylonians had withdrawn. Zedekiah sent his servants to the prophet to say, "Pray now unto the LORD our God for us". Would the Babylonians return? The answer was quite categorical: "The Chaldeans shall come again, and fight against this city, and take it, and burn it with fire" (verse 8). Jeremiah attempted to return to his own land during the respite, but was arrested as a traitor. The princes put Jeremiah in the dungeon but Zedekiah took him out, "and the king asked him secretly in his house, and said, Is there any word from the LORD?" Zedekiah was a secret seeker after God, frightened to reveal his interest in the Word of God lest his ministers should hear of it. We may look with disdain at the weakness of character of such a man, but how many times do we hide our light under a bushel, reluctant to admit to worldly company our association with Christ? "For whosoever shall be ashamed of me and of my words, of him shall the Son of man be ashamed, when he shall come in his own glory, and in his Father's, and of the holy angels" (Luke 9:26).

Zedekiah with some compassion acceded to Jeremiah's request not to return him to the dungeon, and instructed his servants to keep Jeremiah in the court of the prison and to give him his daily bread so long as there was bread to eat (verse 21). But no sooner had the princes heard what sort of message Jeremiah was preaching and sought the death of the prophet, than Zedekiah capitulated to their wishes: "Then Zedekiah the king said, Behold, he is in your hand: for the king is not he that can do any thing against you" (38:4,5). Jeremiah was cast into the pit and "sunk in the mire". It was the intervention of Ebed-Melech which saved Jeremiah's life when he pleaded before the king. How many times would Zedekiah change his mind, or did he indeed have a mind of his own? This time Ebed-Melech was allowed to deliver Jeremiah from the pit. Then Zedekiah took Jeremiah aside into a private location, "the third entry that is in the house of the LORD", no doubt in the shadow of the doorway, or hiding behind a pillar in the twilight zone; and he asked Jeremiah to tell it all: "hide nothing from me". "Zedekiah the king sware secretly unto Jeremiah, saying, As the LORD liveth, that made us this soul, I will not put thee to death, neither will

I give thee into the hand of these men that seek thy life" (verses 14-16).

Fear of Ridicule

Zedekiah's problem was fearfulness, and it can be our problem too. He consulted Jeremiah in secret because he feared his princes. He would not obey the word of Jeremiah to "go forth unto the king of Babylon's princes" because, as he said, "I am afraid of the Jews that are fallen to the Chaldeans, lest they deliver me into their hand, and they mock me". He got Jeremiah to agree to deny the conversation he had with the king if the princes should cross-examine him because of the same fear (38:19,25).

This fear of being laughed at can be a major factor in our reluctance to stand up for the things of God, particularly when we are young, when we are so concerned about our image in the eyes of others. There were those in the time of the Lord Jesus who had the same problem, although the threat to them of excommunication was certainly more significant than the embarrassment which we can be so concerned to avoid: "Among the chief rulers also many believed on him: but because of the Pharisees they did not confess him, lest they should be put out of the synagogue: for they loved the praise of men more than the praise of God" (John 12:42,43). The Lord's appeal to these secret believers was to come out of the twilight into the clear light of day: "He that believeth on me, believeth not on me, but on him that sent me. And he that seeth me seeth him that sent me. I am come a light into the world, that whosoever believeth on me should not abide in darkness" (verses 44-46). If we see the Light and believe on the Light, then we must become light and let it shine before men.

18

"O JERUSALEM, JERUSALEM"

JUST twenty-two years after the death of Josiah the
nation of Judah was in a hopeless and spiritually
terminal condition. For although the reforms of that
great king had indeed encouraged some of the people to
take up the covenant of the Lord with earnest zeal, the
majority of the people had merely paid lip service to the
reforms. The telling observation, which could be made
only by the One who looks on the heart, was this: "Judah
hath not turned unto me with her whole heart, but
feignedly, saith the LORD" (Jeremiah 3:10). No sooner had
Josiah passed off the scene than his faithless sons,
princes, priests and prophets promoted a counter-
reformation which completely overturned the good which
Josiah had accomplished.

There is a very terrible picture of this reversal in the
vision of Ezekiel 8 in which the prophet, through a "hole
in the wall", was shown what was going on in Jerusalem.
He saw on the inner walls of the house of God "every form
of creeping things, and abominable beasts, and all the
idols of the house of Israel" (verse 10). There were to be
found seventy of the elders of the nation. The lamps,
representative of the Word of God, could not have been
alight because it was dark. What were they doing, "every
man in the chambers of his imagery" (verse 12)? These
were "ancient" men who had lived through the great
reforms of Josiah. They had probably been in his presence
many times when the newly discovered Word of God had
been read and expounded. They would have joined with
Josiah in the newly re-established worship of the One
True God in the repaired and renovated temple. But now
they argued that Yahweh had deserted His city. They said,
"The LORD seeth us not; the LORD hath forsaken the earth"
(verse 12). They viewed Yahweh as just another of the city
or state gods who might be deposed from his throne by an

invading army, supported by a more powerful god such as Marduk, chief god of Babylon.

There is no reason to doubt that what Ezekiel saw by vision was a depiction of what the spiritual leaders of the nation had actually done to the the house of Yahweh. But the language of the prophets does cause us to question ourselves about the images which may, from time to time, be painted on the walls of our minds by our own imagination or by the vivid imagery of the media. Such images can be more like engravings than paintings, as judged by the difficulty we may have in removing them from our thoughts. Paul says, "Ye are the temple of the living God" (2 Corinthians 6:16) and goes on to exhort us to "cleanse ourselves from all filthiness of the flesh and spirit, perfecting holiness in the fear of God" (7:1); "casting down imaginations, and every high thing that exalteth itself against the knowledge of God, and bringing into captivity every thought to the obedience of Christ" (10:5).

Worse than Sodom!

One of the most startling descriptions of the state of Judah at this time is the repeated reference to them being worse than Sodom. The book of the Law which Josiah had found predicted that Judah would be overthrown as Sodom was (Deuteronomy 29:23-25). The reason for that was, "their vine is of the vine of Sodom, and of the fields of Gomorrah" (32:32), meaning that their fruits were the worst sort of the works of the flesh. The Lord says through Jeremiah, "I have seen also in the prophets of Jerusalem an horrible thing: they commit adultery, and walk in lies: they strengthen also the hands of evildoers, that none doth return from his wickedness: they are all of them unto me as Sodom, and the inhabitants thereof as Gomorrah" (23:14).

Jeremiah points up the fact that the wickedness was rooted in the prophets, those who claimed to expound the Word of God but misled the people. Not even that applied to Sodom, and so in a significant way Jerusalem was worse than Sodom. Ezekiel the prophet explains this startling conclusion in the parable of chapter 16. Jerusalem, Samaria and Sodom are sisters; all three are bad but Jerusalem is the worst. To Jerusalem the prophet addresses these words, "As I live, saith the Lord GOD, Sodom thy sister hath not done, she nor her daughters, as thou hast done, thou and thy daughters ... Thou also, which hast judged thy sisters, bear thine own shame for thy sins that thou hast committed more abominable than they: they are more righteous than thou: yea, be thou confounded also, and bear thy shame, in that thou hast justified thy sisters" (verses 48,52). Jerusalem had added to the sins of Sodom the covering of hypocrisy. She had rejected the prophets of Yahweh, and despised the Word of God. Because of this, her punishment would be even greater than Sodom's. Jeremiah says: "For the punishment of the iniquity of the daughter of my people is greater than the punishment of the sin of Sodom, that was overthrown as in a moment, and no hands stayed on her" (Lamentations 4:6). Jerusalem's punishment was not quick and clean as was Sodom's, but she had to endure the terrible anguish of the siege, the destruction of the temple and the exile in Babylon.

Returning to the parable of Ezekiel 16 there is another point of great significance. The prophet speaks of the time when the Lord says, "When I shall bring again their captivity, the captivity of Sodom and her daughters, and the captivity of Samaria and her daughters, then will I bring again the captivity of thy captives in the midst of them: that thou mayest bear thine own shame, and mayest be confounded in all that thou hast done, in that thou art a comfort unto them" (verses 53,54). What can this mean? When will Sodom be brought back from captivity, and when will Sodom and her daughters return to their former estate (verse 55)? Surely this can only mean one thing, the resurrection from the dead. Will there be representatives from Sodom and Samaria and Jerusalem at the judgement seat of Christ, and is the passage saying that in that day when the comparison is made between Jerusalem and Sodom, Sodom will take comfort from being less odious in the sight of the judge than Jerusalem?

Is not this the situation described by the Lord Jesus himself when he said of the cities which rejected him, "It shall be more tolerable for Sodom and Gomorrha in the day of judgment, than for that city" (Mark 6:11)? Interestingly, this statement of the Lord in Mark's record is in the chapter which, like Ezekiel 16, describes a woman, Herodius, and her daughter, who together epitomised the wickedness of the nation. The similarity of contexts and the words of the Lord would suggest that he was deliberately drawing a parallel between Jerusalem in his time and the city which was fit only to be overthrown.

An Incurable Disease

The parallels between Jerusalem in the time of Zedekiah and in the time of Christ are highlighted when we compare the last chapter of 2 Chronicles with the comments of the Lord about his day. The awful summary of 2 Chronicles 36 is this:

"Moreover all the chief of the priests, and the people, transgressed very much after all the abominations of the heathen; and polluted the house of the LORD which he had hallowed in Jerusalem. And the LORD God of their fathers sent to them by his messengers, rising up betimes, and sending: because he had compassion on his people, and on his dwelling place: but they mocked the messengers of God, and despised his words, and misused his prophets, until the wrath of the LORD arose against his people, till there was no remedy."

(verses 14-16)

The longsuffering of the Lord in repeatedly sending his prophets to the nation defies human understanding.

Many times this point is emphasised by the prophets with words such as: "I have even sent unto you all my servants the prophets, daily rising up early and sending them" (Jeremiah 7:25). Could they not see the compassion of God, new every morning, in the pleadings of the prophets to turn from the way which would surely lead to destruction? But they laughed off the warnings until there was nothing more that God could do to bring the nation to repentance. They were beyond remedy, or as the Hebrew means in 2 Chronicles 36:16, until there was no healing.

The Lord Jesus found the same situation in his day, and makes appeal to the terrible history of the nation stained with the blood of the prophets. He reminds them that they were the children of those who killed the prophets

155

(Matthew 23:31) and then says: "Wherefore, behold, I send unto you prophets, and wise men, and scribes: and some of them ye shall kill and crucify; and some of them shall ye scourge in your synagogues, and persecute them from city to city: that upon you may come all the righteous blood shed upon the earth" (23:34,35). Then comes the moving appeal to the generation which had refused a greater than Josiah: "O Jerusalem, Jerusalem, thou that killest the prophets, and stonest them which are sent unto thee, how often would I have gathered thy children together, even as a hen gathereth her chickens under her wings, and ye would not! Behold, your house is left unto you desolate" (verses 37,38). The whole of this part of the Lord's discourse with the scribes and Pharisees is based upon 2 Chronicles 36, and when the Lord says, "Behold, your house is left unto you desolate", he is taking up the words of Jeremiah 22:5: "But if ye will not hear these words, I swear by myself, saith the LORD, that this house shall become a desolation."

To drive home the lessons from the times of Josiah and his children the Lord had, after cleansing the temple, told the people a parable which is also based upon the history of ill treatment of the prophets at the hands of the nation. It was the parable of the householder who planted a vineyard, set husbandmen over it and then sent his servants to seek the fruit of the vineyard: "And the husbandmen took his servants, and beat one, and killed another, and stoned another. Again, he sent other servants more than the first: and they did unto them likewise" (Matthew 21:35,36). The chief priests and Pharisees understood exactly what the Lord was referring to (verse 45) and must also have understood what he was implying when he added, "But last of all he sent unto them his son, saying, They will reverence my son" (verse 37). We have before suggested that the rulers of the nation knew that Jesus was the heir to the throne of David, so that even if they did not believe he was literally the Son of God, there was a real force in the words which describe their reaction to the Lord: "This is the heir; come, let us kill him, and let us seize on his inheritance" (verse 38).

The Placebo Effect

One characteristic of the nation at this time of terminal decline is described in the book of Deuteronomy and repeated eight times in the prophecy of Jeremiah. Deuteronomy describes the person who, knowing the judgement of God on idolatry, would respond in this way: "… and it come to pass, when he heareth the words of this curse, that he bless himself in his heart, saying, I shall have peace, though I walk in the imagination of mine heart, to add drunkenness to thirst" (Deuteronomy 29:19). The Hebrew word translated "imagination" is used only ten times in Scripture and the eight occurrences in Jeremiah (3:17; 7:24; 9:14; 11:8; 13:10; 16:12; 18:12; 23:17) make a powerful point. It was the generation of Josiah's children which, having been shown the Scriptures with all the freshness of a new discovery, determined to take no notice and instead to follow unrighteousness with even more enthusiasm.

The sort of person referred to in Deuteronomy took comfort in the thought that he would have "peace" even though the Word of God pronounced wrath. To understand how this mentality could have come about we need to consider the malign influence of the false prophets of Judah who claimed to speak the Word of the Lord, but who in fact were deceivers of the worst sort. We have to realise that Jeremiah was just one of many in Jerusalem who claimed to speak the Word of the Lord, each one claiming to have the Truth and most agreeing with each other about what the king should do. It would be very much as we find ourselves today as Christadelphians. In the eyes of the average person we are just one of many possible churches to choose from, but less attractive than most because we are out of step with the others, emphasising correctness of belief and requiring a radically different approach to life. Then as now it would take a thoughtful, honest seeker after truth to take the time and effort to discern the true from the false. How might Josiah's sons have comforted themselves by relying on other prophets who made the same claims as Jeremiah and Ezekiel, but who spoke much more appealing words. How easy it is today for people to tour the churches and find one which

157

suits them rather than find the one which teaches the truth of the Scriptures.

False prophets could not be recognised by a superficial examination. All prophets, true and false, were claiming to speak "Thus saith the LORD". So how could they be distinguished? First of all it is quite clear that the false prophets were more popular than true prophets: "The prophets prophesy falsely, and the priests bear rule by their means; and my people love to have it so" (Jeremiah 5:31). So the argument today which says that as the evangelical churches are growing rapidly, they must have something right about them is unconvincing. The popularity of the false prophets is explained by their message: "They have healed also the hurt of the daughter of my people slightly, saying, Peace, peace; when there is no peace" (6:14). This is highly significant. The nation was suffering a serious disease and about to lapse into the incurable and terminal phase, but the prophets were offering only a placebo treatment. It was like putting a plaster to cover over a cancer. The problem might be hidden, and the patient thereby feel better, but by not dealing with the problem it could not be cured. This is the false reassurance which so many people trust in today, believing that one way or another, whichever church is right, they will be saved in the end. After all, they say, God is merciful. But the merciful God has revealed His will in the Scriptures and He expects us to allow His Word to make the true diagnosis of our condition, and then to follow the curative remedy.

A most vivid account of false prophets is given in Jeremiah 23: "Hearken not unto the words of the prophets that prophesy unto you: they make you vain: they speak a vision of their own heart, and not out of the mouth of the LORD. They say still unto them that despise me, The LORD hath said, Ye shall have peace: and they say unto every one that walketh in the imagination of his own heart, No evil shall come upon you" (verses 16,17). This passage links the stubbornness of the people, as predicted in Deuteronomy 29, with the role of the false prophets. These prophets claimed to be speaking the word of Yahweh. Did they really believe that or were they consciously deceiving the people? There certainly were prophets who were involved in a grand deception in order to gain materially (23:14).

Perhaps there were others who were deceiving themselves, interpreting their dreams as if they were messages from heaven. The effect was to teach the people the opposite of the truth. Whereas the Lord was saying through Jeremiah and Ezekiel that the nation would go into captivity because of their sins, the false prophets were assuring the people that they would not: "I have heard what the prophets said, that prophesy lies in my name, saying, I have dreamed, I have dreamed. How long shall this be in the heart of the prophets that prophesy lies? yea, they are prophets of the deceit of their own heart; which think to cause my people to forget my name by their dreams which they tell every man to his neighbour" (23:25-27).

The modern counterparts to these prophets are not hard to find. So many churches and religious movements are based upon new "visions" and not on the Scriptures. The Mormons are an obvious example, but even in the mainstream churches the charismatics and evangelicals so often claim to have personal dreams and messages from God. They believe that the Holy Spirit is working directly within them, quite apart from any influence of the Scriptures. In this teaching they deceive the people, because when we test their claims and their doctrines by the Word we see that they are in fact contradicting the plain teaching of Scripture. Certainly their message is often more appealing, but the warning of the times of Josiah's children must be kept in mind. "Peace, peace, when there is no peace" may make us feel better for a while, but it will not cure our problems.

The comparison between the true and the false prophets is likened in the same prophecy of Jeremiah to the difference between chaff and wheat: "What is the chaff to the wheat? saith the LORD" (verse 28). Chaff is light and easily blown about by the wind whereas the solid grain is heavy but lasting. The message of the evangelicals may be light and easy but it is insubstantial. It may not demand much from the audience and may carry them along on a

159

contrived wind of emotions, but the apostle warns us to be "no more children, tossed to and fro, and carried about with every wind of doctrine, by the sleight of men, and cunning craftiness, whereby they lie in wait to deceive" (Ephesians 4:14). The truth is "wheat", but this raw grain has to be worked on by milling in order to become digestible. In other words, we have to apply effort to understanding the Scriptures in order to gain the benefit. If all we are willing to accept is an easy emotionalism we shall not get the nutrition we need to grow spiritually. Consider the following words: "Behold, I am against them that prophesy false dreams, saith the LORD, and do tell them, and cause my people to err by their lies, and by their lightness" (23:32). The people were deceived by the "lightness" of the false prophets. The word in the Hebrew carries the idea of 'bubbling as boiling water' (Strong's Concordance). We might describe such religious leaders as charismatic, and their style of preaching and worship as effervescent. They would claim that they are being moved by the Spirit of God, and that the joy of their gatherings is an expression of the Spirit working through them. Many are deceived by such claims – they have mass appeal.

But so did the false prophets of Jeremiah's day. The Christadelphians look outdated, narrow-minded, unyielding and dry – so did Jeremiah. In the end the false prophets were shown up for what they really were. Jerusalem was captured and the nation did suffer terribly. Jeremiah was proved right. But by then it was too late for that generation. They had been fooled by an easy and light message which appealed to the flesh. The parallels with our day are obvious. It may be argued that the brotherhood is not as enthusiastic as it should be about the great truths we understand, and that the zeal of brethren and sisters is waning. And that may be true in some parts of the ecclesial world. But the answer cannot be to seek the way of the false prophets. Rather let us return to the "wheat" of God's Word, to the "wholesome words, even the words of our Lord Jesus Christ, and to the doctrine which is according to godliness" (1 Timothy 6:3).

19

SHALL WE LEARN THE LESSONS?

THE day of the Lord will come! They could not believe it would happen. When Jeremiah predicted the impending destruction of the city the people challenged him to prove it: "Behold, they say unto me, Where is the word of the LORD? Let it come now" (Jeremiah 17:15). When Ezekiel confirmed these prophecies they recited the proverb: "The days are prolonged, and every vision faileth" (Ezekiel 12:22), and also said, "The vision that he seeth is for many days to come, and he prophesieth of the times that are far off" (verse 27). But the vision did not fail: "In the fifth month, on the seventh day of the month, which is the nineteenth year of king Nebuchadnezzar king of Babylon, came Nebuzaradan, captain of the guard, a servant of the king of Babylon, unto Jerusalem: and he burnt the house of the LORD" (2 Kings 25:8,9).

It was the same in the first century when the apostles' warning of the destruction of Jerusalem went unheeded by the majority. The Lord Jesus Christ said that generation would not pass away until all was fulfilled. Included in his prophecy were the grim words: "And they shall fall by the edge of the sword, and shall be led away captive into all nations: and Jerusalem shall be trodden down of the Gentiles, until the times of the Gentiles be fulfilled" (Luke 21:24). The nation scoffed: "Where is the promise of his coming? for since the fathers fell asleep, all things continue as they were from the beginning of the creation" (2 Peter 3:4). But less than 40 years after the Lord uttered the Olivet prophecy the Roman legions under Titus razed Jerusalem and the second temple.

And now we must ask ourselves whether we shall be any different. The lessons from the life and times of Josiah and his children, and the lessons from the last days of

161

Judah's commonwealth, are all the more powerful for us because of the parallels between those times and our own. We too are living at the end of an epoch. The fig tree of Israel has begun to shoot forth and we know that summer is nigh. The restoration of Israel to their land, the freeing of Jerusalem from Gentile control, and the cry of "peace and security" in the Middle East all signal the nearness of the coming of the Lord. But will our generation be any better prepared for that day than were the last generations of Josiah's children and Judah's commonwealth? Are we a "nation bringing forth the fruits" (Matthew 21:43)? "When the Son of man cometh, shall he find faith on the earth?" (Luke 18:8).

They would not listen!

The reasons for the disaster of 587 BC are summarised in Nehemiah 9: "Yet many years didst thou forbear them, and testifiedst against them by thy spirit in thy prophets: yet would they not give ear: therefore gavest thou them into the hand of the people of the lands ... Neither have our kings, our princes, our priests, nor our fathers, kept thy law, nor hearkened unto thy commandments and thy testimonies, wherewith thou didst testify against them. For they have not served thee in their kingdom, and in thy great goodness that thou gavest them" (verses 30,34,35). It was their stubbornness in refusing to hear God's Word for which they were held responsible. And the Lord Jesus says to his disciples: "He that rejecteth me, and receiveth not my words, hath one that judgeth him: the word that I have spoken, the same shall judge him in the last day" (John 12:48).

In addition to the rejection of the Truth by Jeremiah's contemporaries, the people clung on to the words of false prophets whose message was far more palatable, and whose style was light and easy to listen to. Their message was that the way of life of the people was fine, they need not change their ways, and God would not bring judgement upon them as Jeremiah declared would happen. In saying these things they wrongly divided the Word of truth and "stole" God's words from the people (Jeremiah 23:30). Falsification of the text of Scripture was part of their method (Jeremiah 8:8). Some of these

162

prophets made short term prophecies about the return of Jehoiachin's captivity from Babylon (28:1-4). But such wishful thinking was not a characteristic the people should have expected of a prophet speaking the truth. Jeremiah observed: "The prophets that have been before me and before thee of old prophesied both against many countries, and against great kingdoms, of war, and of evil, and of pestilence. The prophet which prophesieth of peace, when the word of the prophet shall come to pass, then shall the prophet be known, that the LORD hath truly sent him" (verses 8,9). The point here was that false prophets speak what the people are inclined to hear, but true prophets tell it as it is. How careful we must be to seek the accuracy of God's Word in order that we might learn the mind of God. We dare not choose our teachers on the basis of the palatability of their message or their easy-to-listen-to style. The only criterion which really matters in the end is the scriptural soundness of their words.

"There is a generation that curseth their father"

Nehemiah made reference to "our kings, our princes" as those who had rejected the Word of God. These were the children of Josiah, and they had been brought up in the time of the rediscovery of the Word. During the reign of Josiah the nation "departed not from following the LORD, the God of their fathers" (2 Chronicles 34:33), but as soon as he died his sons embarked upon reigns of idolatry and licentiousness which their father could never have tolerated. The only explanation for this dramatic reversal of the spiritual state of Judah is that these young men, even during their father's reign, and despite his wonderful example of zeal and faithfulness, privately despised the things of the Truth and were merely biding their time until they could have their freedom.

Jehoahaz was the first to succeed Josiah at the age of 23 years, and in a reign of just three months he acquired a reputation for doing evil in the sight of the Lord. It seems that he, with his brothers, had followed the fashion in their teenage years, as indicated by their uncle Zephaniah who described the "king's children" as those "clothed in strange (foreign) apparel" (1:8). Here is a warning, especially for our young people today, to beware the

163

fashions of worldliness which are geared to a freedom which really is slavery to sin. When the Lord returns he will expect all of us to be clothed with appropriate "wedding garments" of faithfulness and righteousness.

Jehoahaz was followed by his elder brother Jehoiakim whose eleven year reign is remembered for his exploitation of the poor and needy (Jeremiah 22:15-17). He was a king who revelled in the luxury of palace life, but ignored the weighty responsibilities of his position. Jehoiakim bolstered himself against the words of Jeremiah by surrounding himself with worldly friends (26:21). When the Word of God was read aloud in his hearing, he systematically cut up the pages of the scroll with his penknife and threw them into the fire (chapter 36). Any man who can treat God's Word in that way should expect the treatment which Jehoiakim suffered at the hands of the Babylonians.

Jehoiakim's son Jehoiachin, who then took the throne as a young man of eighteen, was unworthy to bear the name he had been given in the reign of Josiah. He was known to some as Jeconiah, although Jeremiah will only call him Coniah, leaving out the "Yah" of God's memorial name. In the Scriptures Jehoiachin is likened to a vessel which is despised and broken and therefore unfit for use (Jeremiah 22:28). He was a king who did not have the qualifications for kingship, a "signet" ring which did not have the weight to bear responsibility (verse 24). The powerful lessons for us which come from his reign are brought out by the Apostle Paul when he writes to Timothy about the vessels "unto honour" which are "meet for the master's use, and prepared unto every good work". These vessels, he says, have to be purged from dishonour, and he immediately goes on to exhort Timothy to "flee also youthful lusts" (2 Timothy 2:21,22).

The last prince to sit on Josiah's throne was Zedekiah, Josiah's youngest son. More space is given to this man than to his brothers, perhaps because there was more to him and at least some semblance of respect in him for the Word of God. His problem was his vacillation, swinging between right and wrong. He made an oath before God, but broke it soon after (2 Chronicles 36:13). During the siege of Jerusalem he rightly instituted the "year of release" when all the bondservants were set free, but no sooner had the siege temporarily lifted than the servants were taken back into slavery (Jeremiah 34:11). During the siege Zedekiah secretly enquired of the Lord through Jeremiah, but he was afraid to be seen by his courtiers (38:25). He wanted Jeremiah to pray for him, but not to tell his friends. He is depicted by Ezekiel as walking into captivity "in the twilight" (Ezekiel 12:7), and this sums up the man. He was living in a twilight, unable to come completely into the light of God's way. He was a half-hearted hearer and not a doer of the Word. And there is much we can learn from this man. Fearfulness of ridicule causes us to hide in shadowy places, neither one thing nor the other. We need to come out into the light and then we shall find strength from the Lord.

What will their father think?

In the resurrection, what will Josiah think when he learns what happened to his children? Will he be surprised, or was it evident from the experiences he had with his boys that this is the way their minds were set from an early age? Josiah certainly knew that the kingdom was to go into rapid and terminal decline (2 Kings 22:16). He knew that he was to be spared the ordeal of witnessing the judgements which his grandfather Manasseh brought upon the nation. But he also knew from the experience of his grandfather that even rebellious and vilely wicked young men can turn to God and find forgiveness. The way in which the Lord dealt with Manasseh is one of the most amazing events in Scripture, manifesting a power to forgive which is far beyond the reach of man's understanding.

When Josiah has to give account, it will be an account of a life lived faithfully. Josiah had set his sons the best example. At the age of sixteen his first priority was to seek the Kingdom of God and His righteousness. Despite the poor example of his father and grandfather he rose above their influences. Many would have made excuses for waywardness by blaming their upbringing, but Josiah made his own choice to follow the right way. Josiah's path had been prophesied years before by the "man of God" who spoke of the one called Josiah who would overturn the idolatry which Jeroboam had set up in Bethel. And how did Josiah fulfil that prediction? Travelling through the land he broke down every symbol of idolatry and crushed it to powder or burned it to ash. It is what each one of us has to do in our own lives with a similar zeal. Bethel and the other high places represented the apostasy from the Truth, in which the doctrines of idolatry are married with the language of the Truth, and in so doing the character of God is blasphemed. It was the exact equivalent of what the churches today have done with the Bible, keeping the names of God and of the Lord Jesus Christ, but associating them with pagan philosophies. The worship which they practised at those high places made them despicable dens of vice, and this was swept away by Josiah.

Having gone through the land, Josiah found that the temple had once more been polluted by idols and a second cleansing was required. Not only that, but the fabric of the building was badly in need of repair. In setting about this work he demonstrated the balance which we all need to have in our own lives, a combination of removing that which offends and replacing it with the positive things of God. Josiah sought helpers in this work from all the people, including the remnant from the north who were invited back to Jerusalem to worship. It is said that "the men did the work faithfully" (2 Chronicles 34:12) and this in itself is the perfect combination. Faith without works is dead, and works without faith is futile. The work was done faithfully by all concerned, the overseers, the skilled craftsmen and the labourers. Of particular interest is the fact that the management of the labourers was carried out by the temple musicians! They worked effectively because the guiding influence was praise to God.

As the work was underway the most dramatic discovery was made: the original copy of the book of the Law – probably the only surviving copy. Its discovery was the centrepiece of this period and was of enormous historical significance. It ensured the continuance of the Word of God, in the hands of the people. That it was the original copy was the perfect answer to the false representations of

Scripture which seem to have been in circulation (Jeremiah 8:8,9). When Josiah heard it read he was dismayed by the curses of Deuteronomy. His diligence to find out how he should respond, and his single-minded dedication to obeying the Word were Josiah's greatest qualities. He "turned not aside to the right hand or to the left". Making his own copy of the Law as was required of a king, he made the Word of God his own, and so should we. So easily that Word can be lost in our homes when we fail to see its true worth, and it can be lost in our ecclesias when the word of exhortation, the Bible Class and the gospel proclamation are reduced to men's opinions and philosophies.

The prophet Jeremiah was sent by God to reinforce the lessons from the newly discovered Word. His prophecy is full of references back to Deuteronomy, the book which was to be laid up next to the ark as a witness to later generations. Jeremiah's work completed the witness by drawing attention to what their God had predicted would happen, both with respect to their waywardness and God's judgements upon them. And they could not say that they did not know these things, because the very scroll written by Moses was there to be seen and heard.

The Word discovered led Josiah to enter into a new covenant with the Lord, and though the nation's heart was not in it, the lesson for us is plain. The Word of God, once understood, commands our response. Josiah responded "with all his heart, and with all his soul, and with all his might" (2 Kings 23:25). Half-heartedness is an unacceptable offering. The new covenant was followed by a more intensive cleansing of idolatry, not just the larger images and the places of worship but also now the private household gods, as Jerusalem was searched with candles (Zephaniah 1:12). And there was a tremendous energy brought to bear. Josiah ran as he did the work, so disgusted was he with the things which polluted the house of God.

Josiah was a man in a hurry. There was so much to do and so little time left. But why? The answer is that he was aiming to keep the passover in the first month at the right time. Everything had to be in order. No short cuts were to be taken. They did it "according to the word of the LORD by the hand of Moses" (2 Chronicles 35:6), but only because of careful preparation (verse 4) and the fact that everyone concerned pulled their weight and more (verse 14). It was all done in the spirit of Habakkuk: "Write the vision, and make it plain upon tables, that he may run that readeth it" (2:2).

The rest of Josiah's reign is barely mentioned except for the final act when he went out against Pharaoh-Necho and was killed. But we are given an insight into the beauty of his character. His lovingkindness is the one characteristic specified in the historical record, and Jeremiah amplifies this when he refers to Josiah judging the cause of the poor and the needy – "Was not this to know me? saith the LORD" (Jeremiah 22:16). Josiah knew Yahweh by learning and living the Truth. In so doing he developed a character which was in measure a reflection of the divine. And inasmuch as he did this, he foreshadowed the Lord Jesus Christ himself.

The Word made Flesh

The Lord Jesus must surely have derived comfort and strength from Josiah, particularly during the last week of his ministry. As the Lord rode into Jerusalem he knew he was going to have to cleanse the temple again, as did Josiah. When the rulers asked him by what authority he did this, it seems that even they recognised the pattern of kingship he was following. He prevented them carrying vessels through the temple, as did Josiah, and he quoted the words of Jeremiah from exactly that same period of Jerusalem's history – "Ye have made it a den of thieves". During that week he spoke parables which in part at least were taken from the times of Josiah: the man who came to the wedding without the proper attire; the husbandmen who mistreated the prophets of God down through the centuries. The stone at which they stumbled would crush to powder those enemies, as Josiah had crushed the idols of his generation. During that week they challenged him to say what the greatest commandment was. It was none other than the commandment honoured uniquely in the life of Josiah, to love the Lord with their "all". And how well the application of that principle was exemplified by the poorest amongst them, the widow who gave to God "all that she had, even all her living". If only they realised it, there in the treasury of the house of God was the Word asking to be discovered, as it had been in the days of Josiah. Like Josiah, the Lord then established a new covenant and instituted a new passover. He prepared his house; he provided the lamb. Josiah was unique in his own era, but there had never been one like this, nor afterwards could there be another.

But the question for us now is what will become of his children living in the last generation of Gentile times? Shall we be like Jehoahaz or Jehoiakim, Jehoiachin or Zedekiah? Or shall we be like Daniel, Hananiah, Mishael and Azariah, Jeremiah and Ezekiel, people who were brought up in that same generation with the same range of influences bearing in upon them, but who chose a better way? Daniel was born at about the time the book of the Law was discovered. He would have been a young teenager when Josiah died. Around him were the true prophets like Jeremiah and Zephaniah, but also the false prophets and the wayward princes. Which rôle model would he choose? By the age probably of only 16 years he had already developed a faith which refused the delicacies of Babylon. He was fearless in speaking God's Word, even when the message was harsh and its target was the most powerful man in the world. His life was lived in isolation with just the Word of God and perhaps a few like-minded friends to comfort him, and the visions of God to inspire him. He was a man of prayer who sought the peace of Jerusalem three times a day! His place in the Kingdom of God is assured. And when Daniel stands in his lot at the end of days, he will find himself alongside the one who must surely have been his inspiration in the days of his youth. And what feelings of gratitude will Daniel have in his heart in that day when they, together with the faithful of all generations, behold the face of the greatest Son of David, the Son of God!

JOSIAH AND HIS CHILDREN

INDEX OF SCRIPTURE REFERENCES

Genesis
17:7 74
41:42 135
48:14 118
Exodus
12:3 103
:11 105
:15 . . . . 106, 107
:19 106
13:7 106
15: 51
:17 50
32:20 38
34:6,7 . . . . . 14, 108
Leviticus
17:7 88
18:21 90
20:2 90
:3 90
:4,5 90
21:16-24 87
26:1 43
Numbers
4:3 49
:23 49
15:38,39 120
Deuteronomy
4:15,19 82
:33,36 125
5:24,26 125
:29 125
6:4 61
:5 119
:7 119
7:5 38

10:17,18. 109
14:29 110
15: 111
:7,8 110
16: 100
:1 99
:4 . . . . . . 99, 106
:11 110
:14 110
17: 66
:11 66
:12 . . . . . . 66, 67
:18 84
:18,19 67
:20 67
18:18 68
24:16 57
:21 110
27:5,6 57
:8 72
:9 73
:26 . 57, 73, 75, 76
28: 1, 57
:15,45 67
:20 67
29: 158
:1 72
:12,13 74
:19 157
:21-29 75
:23-25 153
30:2 75
:6 . . . . . 75, 77, 79
:9 75
:10 . . . . . . 75, 77

:11-14 75
:15,16 78
:19,20 116
31:18,20 67
:24-26 57
32:32 153
Joshua
8:31 57
:34 57
24:25,26 58
1 Samuel
15:22 125
1 Kings
11:7 90
12:28 30
:32,33 30
13: 29, 30
:2 . . . . . . 31, 115
:5 31
:6 32
:9 33
:18 33
:21,22 34
:30 133
2 Kings
12:15 52
14:6 57
17:16 9
18:5,6 2
20:5 28
:5,6 28
21:2 9
:3 . . . . . . 9, 83, 95
:4-8 10
21:9-11 11

2 Kings – *continued*

21:12-15 12
:16 11
:17 27
:22 20
22: 39, 66
:1 23
:2 1, 27, 28, 67, 89
:4 45
:5 49
:6 48
:7 52
:8 57
:11 . . . . 1, 54
:13 . . . . . . 63, 64
:14 84
:15. 66
:15,16 64
:16 165
:17 115
:18 64
:19,20 64
23: 76, 115
:1 82
:1,2 72
:2 . . . . 79, 82, 115
:3 . . . . 77, 82
:4 . . . . 39, 82, 115
:5 . . . . 40, 85
:5-14 96
:6 85
:7 86
:8 88
:9 87
:10 91
:11 93
:12 37, 94, 96, 104
:13 . . . . . . 88, 94
:14 95
:17,18 29
:18 66
:21 99
:24 . . . . 39, 41, 81,
97,107

:25 . . . . . 2, 61, 67,
100, 108,
115, 167
:26,27 . . . . 12, 108
:32 . . . . 5, 118
:35 123
24:1 . . . . . 128, 132
:2 131
:3,4 12
:9 134
:10-12 140
:13 142
:19 143
:33 118
25:1-3 145
:4 146
:6 146
:7 147
:8,9 161
:27-30 141

1 Chronicles

3:15 . . . . . 117, 118
:16 135
17:9,10 51
22:5 48
29:23 123

2 Chronicles

11:14 34
:17 28
15:16 38
30:2 100
:6-8 138
:22 100
31:1 38
:4 100
32:32 109
33:11-13 13
:15 . . . . . . 21, 94
:15,16 13
:17 13
:18 19
:18,19 27
:19 20
:22 37

:22,23 20
34: 66
:1-3 18
:2 67
:3 . 27, 36, 81, 115
:4 85
:4,5 37
:6 . . . . 38, 81, 115
:7 . . . . 38, 81
:8 . 39, 45, 47, 81,
115
:9 45
:10 47
:11 48
:12 . . . 49, 52, 166
:12,13 53
:13 47
:14 . . . . . . 56, 58
:16-18 63
:27 54
:30 79
:31 77
:32 122
:33 . . . . . 115, 163
35:1 . . . . . 100, 115
:2 100
:3 . . . . 58, 101
:4 168
:5 102
:6 . . . . . . 103, 168
:7 . . 103, 115, 122
:8,9 103
:10-12 104
:13 104
:14 . . . . . 104, 168
:15 . . . . . 104, 106
:16 105
:17 107
:20 . . . . . 112, 115
:22 113
:25 114
:26,27 108
36: 132, 156
:5 . . . . 5, 132

172

:8 133
:9 134
:10 140
:12 . . . . 144, 147
:13 . . . . 144, 164
:14-16 . . . 15, 155
:16 155
:21 144
:22 144
:30 132

Nehemiah
9:30,34,35 162

Psalms
15:1,4 145
69: 42
141:2 31

Proverbs
28:20 52
30:11-14 22

Ecclesiastes
2:1-11 26
12:1 26

Isaiah
38:5 28
66:2 64

Jeremiah
1:6 24
:7-9 68
2:31 56
:35 22
3:10 . . . . 5, 77, 152
:16,17 102
:17 . . . . . 102, 157
5:31 158
6:13 79
:14 158
7:6 59
:9 59
:9,10 . . . . . 89, 92
:11 59
:13 15
:20 91
:24 157
:25 155

:31 91
:32,33 91
8:2 83
:8 162
:8,9 . . . . . 55, 167
:11 55
:12 98
9: 111
:14 157
:23 112
:23,24 . . . 110, 111
10: :3,4,9 49
11:2-4 76
:5 76
:6 76
:8 157
:9,10 77
13:10 157
15:4 . . . . 5, 10
:16 . . . . . . 55, 68
16:12 157
17:15 161
18:6 138
:12 . . . . . 139, 157
:19 68
19:3 91
:11 . . . . . 91, 139
:13 83
21:1,2 148
:5 148
:7 148
:12 148
22: . . . 111, 118, 135
:5 156
:11,12 119
:13 133
:13,14 123
:14,17 133
:15 123
:15-17 29, 124, 164
:16 . . 80, 109, 168
:18,19 133
:21 125
:24 164

:24-27 135
:25 136
:28 . . . . . 136, 164
:29 136
:30 137
23:14 . . . . . 153, 159
:16,17 158
:17 157
:25-27 159
:28 159
:30 162
:32 160
24: 51, 52, 142
:1 50
:5,6 50
25: 128
26:1 127
:2 127
:3 127
:11 127
:12-23 133
:16 127
:21 . . . . . 133, 164
:21-23 128
:24 . . . . . 24, 128
27:12,13 146
28:1-4 163
:4 142
:8,9 163
29: 142
31:9 118
:31-34 78
32:2 149
.35 . . . . . . 90, 91
:37 149
:38 149
33:15 149
34:11 . . . . 145, 165
:15 145
:17 145
:21 145
:22 145
36: . . . 128, 132, 164
:5,6 129

173

JOSIAH AND HIS CHILDREN

Jeremiah – *continued*
36:7 129
:20 129
:23 129
:24. 130
:25 133
37:8 150
:21 150
38:4,5 150
:14-16 151
:19,25 151
:25 165
44:9 126
:17 86
45:3 130
:4,5 131
52:11 147
:31-34 141
Lamentations
2:3,4 114
:11,12 146
3:12,13 114
:27 . . . . . 26, 114
4:6 154
:10 146
5:10 85
Ezekiel
8:10 152
:12 . . . . . 42, 152
12: 148
:4 146
:7 . . . . . 146, 165
:12 147
:13 147
:22 161
:27 161
14:3 43
16: 155
:48,52 154
:53,54 154
:55 154
17:15,16 144
:19 144
18:4 117

19:4 131
:5-9 131
:9 122
21:25 5
:25-27 147
:26,27 137
22:7 22
:25 22
33:31,32 149
36:26 79
44:10-13 87
Daniel
1:3 7
2: 44, 130
9:20-27 16
Hosea
8:8 136
10:5 85
Nahum
3:13,15 3
Habakkuk
1: 97
2: 97
:2 168
:9 98
:11 98
Zephaniah
1: 122
:1 23
:4 85
:4,5 94
:4-6 40
:5 41
:6 41
:7,8 121
:8 . . . . . 119, 163
:12 . . 41, 107, 167
3:7,8 14
Haggai
2:23 137
Zechariah
12:10 79
:10,11 115
13:1,2 115

14: 79
****
Matthew
6:11 155
7:6,7 60
12:35 70
13:44-46 69
:51 69
:52 69
21:23 42
:35,36 156
:37 156
:38 . . . . . 140, 156
:43 162
:43,44 44
:45 156
22:1-14 121
:2,3 121
:4 121
:7 121
:9,10 122
:11,12 122
23: 115
:15 92
:27 96
:31 155
:33 92
:34,35 156
:37,38 156
:38 47
Mark
11:15-17 115
:16 92
:17 59
:32,33 60
:34 60
:40 61
:42 62
:43,44 61
12:10 59
:24 59
:29-31 60
:33 79
:35,36 59
13: 115

174

INDEX OF SCRIPTURE REFERENCES

:2 47
:34,35 47
14:12 105
:15 . . . . 105, 115
:24 115
Luke
1:32 115
2:49 115
9:26 150
11:24-26 46
15: 115
:25 53
16:10 52
18:8 162
19:38 98
:40 98
:41-44 98
21:24 . . . . . 136, 161
22:8 105
:27 105
John
1: 55
:14 . . . . . 109, 115
2: 42
:13-16 115
:14-17 97
12:42,43 151
:44-46 151
:48 162
14:2 . . . . . 113, 115
:2,3 47
Acts
10:38 115
15:14-16 138
17:21 70
Romans
1:30 21
4: 80
10:6 75
12:1 103
15:4 101
1 Corinthians
1:21 111
:26-31 111
:30 112

3:3 107
:6-10 51
:10,11 112
4:2 52
5:7 . . 105, 106, 115
:8 107
13: 112
2 Corinthians
3:3. 80
6:14 148
:15,16 53
:16 153
7:1 153
8:12 62
10:5 153
Galatians
3:10 . . . . . . 57, 73
:11 75
:17 74
6:2 104
Ephesians
2:12 79
:22 51
4:14 160
5:5 42
:8 148
Philippians
2:6 56
:6-11 56
3:14 56
Colossians
2:6,7 51
:21 46
3:22,23 52
:5 . . . . . . 42, 124
:8-12 46
:9,10 122
1 Timothy
1:18 49
3:7 87
:15 89
6: 42
:1 138
:3 160
:3-5 32

:10,11 32
2 Timothy
1:5 7
2: 85
:2 52
:17 70
:20,21 84
:21 139
:21,22 164
:22 139
3:13 21
:14-17 33
4:3 70
:5 49
Titus
1:7 87
Hebrews
3:12 138
10:23 102
:29 133
12:11 139
:15 139
13:15,16 62
James
2:10 73
1 Peter
1:2,19 105
:13 105
:17 105
2:5 51
:21 103
2 Peter
3:4 161
:15 16
:16 65
1 John
2:3-5 110
3:16,17 111
4:8 111
3 John
:5 53
Revelation
3:21 138
14:1 138
17:5 96

JOSIAH AND HIS CHILDREN

SUBJECT INDEX

A

Adad, weather god, 83
Age, at baptism, 25
Aharoni, Y, archaeologist, 123
Altars, of Baalim, 37
Amon, 20-23
Apparel, strange, 121
Archaeological site, Gezer, 36, 37; Ramat Rahel, 123
Asherah, 36,86,95
Ashur-uballit, 3
Assyria, 3
Astarte, goddess of love, 85

B

Babylonians, 143, 145
Baptism, appropriate age for, 25,26
Baruch, 130
Bethel, 30
Book of the Law, 166
British Museum, relics from Sennacherib's palace, 3

C

Carchemish, Battle of, 4, 128
Chariots, of the sun, 93
Chemarim, idolatrous priest, 85
Child sacrifice, 90
Chronological chart, The Last Generation, 6
Classes of workers, 47-53

Cleansing the land, on two occasions, 39, 81
Clothing, dubious fashions, 120; strange apparel, 121
Coniah (see Jehoiachin)
Copy of Law, made by Josiah, 67
Covenant, New, 72-80
Craftsmen, repairing temple 49-52

D

Daniel, and friends, 128, 169
David, 27
Deuteronomy, likely content of discovered scroll, 57
Dress, ribband of blue, 120; strange apparel, 119-122, 163

F

False prophets, 158-160
Fashion, inappropriate, 120
Fear, of ridicule, 151
Finding the Law, 56-62

G

Gate, of Joshua, 88
Gehenna, 92
Generation, Chart of The Last, 6; The Last, 4
Gezer, high place, 36; archaeological site, 36,37

177

H

Hephzibah, 9

Hezekiah, extension of life, 28; uniquely righteous, 2

Hilkiah, 27

Hinnom, Valley of, 90, 92

Huldah, prophetess, 24

I

Idols, ground to powder, 44; present day, 42

Illustration, stela of Ashurna-sirpal, 83

Image, graven, 43

Ishtar, goddess of love and war, 83

J

Jeconiah (see Jehoiachin)

Jedidah, 23

Jehoahaz, 117, 163

Jehoiachin (Jeconiah) (Coniah), 134-142, 164

Jehoiakim, 117, 122-133, 164

Jeroboam, apostasy of, 30, 166

Jeremiah, counsellor and friend, 24; prophecies, 148-150

Jerusalem, 152

Johanan, 117

Josiah, aged 8, 1, 18; compared with Christ, 2; copied Law, 67; died in Jerusalem, 3, 113; foreshadowed Christ, 41, 108-115; meaning of name, 8; mission foretold, 31; reformation of, 1; seeking God, 27; uniquely righteous, 2, 97; wayward sons of, 9; wounded by arrow, 3, 113

K

Kidron Valley, 85, 91

L

Labourers, repairing temple, 53

Last generation (before Babylonian captivity), 4-6; chart, 6

Law, discovered scroll containing Deuteronomy, 57

Leaven, 106

Love and war goddess, Ishtar, 83

Love goddess, Astarte, 85

M

Man of God, prophesying, 32; slain by a lion, 34

Manasseh, forgiveness of, 14, 19; his malign influence, 5; repentance of, 13, 19; wickedness of, 9-12

Mattaniah (see Zedekiah)

Medes and Scythians, 3

Molech, 90

Moon god, Sin, 83

Mordecai, 4, 169

Moses, his original copy of Law, 56

Mount of Corruption, 94

N

Nathan-melech, 93

Nebuchadnezzar, 128, 130, 132, 143, 145

Nineveh, captured by Babylonians and Medes, 3; burned, so fulfilling prophecy, 3

O

Original (Moses') copy of Law, 56

Overseers, work of repairing temple 47-49

Overturning, tables of money-changers, 42

P

Pagan god, Adad, 83; Shamash, 83; Sin, 83

Pagan goddess, Astarte, 85; Ishtar, 83

Parable, Wedding of king's son, 121

Parwar, 93

Passover, Hezekiah's, 100; Josiah's, 99-104; the Lord's, 104

Pharaoh-Necho, 3, 112, 113, 118

Poor widow, 61

Prophecy, Olivet, 161

Prophets, false, 158-160

R

Ramat Rahel, site of excavations, 123

Ridicule, fear of, 151

S

Samaria, 154

Shallum, 25, 117

Shamash, Sun god, 83

Shaphan, the scribe, 1

Sin, the Moon god, 83

Sodom, 153

Sun god, Shamash, 83

Sun, moon and stars, worship of, 83

T

Temple, repairing the, 45-53

Tophet, 91

V

Valley, Kidron, 91; of Hinnom, 90, 92

Vessels, fit for destruction, 81; of honour, 84

Visiting the iniquity of the fathers, 14

W

Weather god, Adad, 83

Word of God, lost and found, 54; made flesh, 59; respect for, 63-71

Workers, classes of, 47-53

Z

Zedekiah (Mattaniah), 117, 143-151, 164

Zephaniah, 23